D0560603

The Observer's Pocket Series

AIRCRAFT

Observer's Books

NATURAL HISTORY
Birds · Birds' Eggs · Wild Animals · Zoo Animals
Farm Animals · Freshwater Fishes · Sea Fishes
Tropical Fishes · Butterflies · Larger Moths
Insects and Spiders · Pond Life · Sea and Seashore
Seashells . Dogs . Horses and Ponies . Cats · Pets
Trees · Wild Flowers · Grasses · Mushrooms
Lichens · Cacti · Garden Flowers · Flowering Shrubs
House Plants · Vegetables · Geology · Fossils
Weather · Astronomy

SPORT
Association Football · Cricket · Golf · Coarse
Fishing · Fly Fishing · Show Jumping
Motor Sport

TRANSPORT
Automobiles · Aircraft · Commercial Vehicles
Motorcycles · Steam Locomotives · Ships · Small
Craft · Manned Spaceflight · Unmanned Spaceflight

ARCHITECTURE
Architecture · Churches · Cathedrals

COLLECTING
Awards and Medals · Coins · Postage Stamps
Glass · Pottery and Porcelain · Firearms

ARTS AND CRAFTS
Music · Painting · Modern Art · Sculpture
Furniture · Sewing

HISTORY AND GENERAL INTEREST
Ancient Britain · Flags · Heraldry · European
Costume

TRAVEL
London · Tourist Atlas GB · Cotswolds and
Shakespeare Country · Lake District

The Observer's Book of
AIRCRAFT

COMPILED BY
WILLIAM GREEN

WITH SILHOUETTES BY
DENNIS PUNNETT

DESCRIBING 138 AIRCRAFT
WITH 245 ILLUSTRATIONS

1978 EDITION

FREDERICK WARNE

Twenty-seventh Edition 1978

LIBRARY OF CONGRESS CATALOG CARD NO: 57 4425

ISBN 0 7232 1577 4

Printed in Great Britain

INTRODUCTION TO THE 1978 EDITION

Twelve months represent a very brief span of time in relation to the annals of aviation, yet they can embrace many changes and developments in the aeronautical scene, and those comprising the year past witnessed their share of aviation highlights. On the commercial side, the prospects of further production of the Concorde become increasingly remote, but the year saw inauguration by the Anglo-French supersonic airliner of services to New York, after a protracted legal battle, and to Singapore, while its Soviet counterpart, the Tu-144, finally initiated services between Moscow and Alma Ata. Boeing's 727, 737 and 747 continued to attract a steady stream of customers, the company delivering its 3,000th commercial jet airliner during the year, and the commercial prospects of Europe's Airbus A300B improved immeasurably. Conversely, the production demise of Federal Germany's VFW 614 short-haul airliner became certain at the year's end and, further down the size scale, the production futures of the extraordinarily successful Britten-Norman Islander and Trislander were in jeopardy owing to the problems of the parent Fairey company.

In so far as business executive aircraft were concerned, sales were buoyant and development vigorous, with a number of new types and new variants of existing types, such as the CL-600 Challenger, Citation II, Falcon 20G, Learjet 28 Longhorn, Sabreliner 65 and Hustler 400, under test or approaching their initial test phase. The year saw expanding use of such aerodynamic developments as supercritical aerofoils (e.g. Falcon 50, Sabreliner 65) and Whitcomb winglets (e.g. Learjet Longhorn, Arava 202), and an increase in popularity of the T-tail configuration for light aircraft (e.g. Beech Duchess and Piper's Cheyenne III, Lance II and Tomahawk).

Two innovatory aircraft that began their test programmes during the course of the year were Rockwell International's XFV-12A of thrust-augmented wing concept and RFB's Fantrainer, which, flown in October, utilises an integrated ducted-fan propulsion system. Apart from the CASA 101 trainer, new military aircraft were most noteworthy for their absence, although such types as the Alpha Jet, the JA 37 Viggen, the Mitsubishi F-1 and Super Étendard all flew in production form for the first time. Military débutantes are likely to be more prolific during 1978, however, as perusal of the following pages will reveal, with flight testing of the Mirage 2000 being anticipated in April, the F-18 Hornet in September and the Super Mirage 4000—details of which had still to be revealed at press date—in October, with two derivatives of the V/STOL Harrier, the Sea Harrier and the AV-8B, being expected to fly around mid-year and year's end respectively.

These newcomers, together with the latest variants of established types, will be found in the pages of this, the 27th annual edition of *The Observer's Book of Aircraft*.   WILLIAM GREEN

AERITALIA G.222

Country of Origin: Italy.

Type: General-purpose military transport.

Power Plant: Two 3,400 shp (derated from 4,400 shp) General Electric T64-P4D turboprops.

Performance: (At max. take-off weight) Max. speed, 336 mph (540 km/h) at 15,000 ft (4 570 m); continuous cruise, 224 mph (360 km/h) at 14,750 ft (4 500 m); range (at optimum altitude and cruise), 435 mls (700 km) with 19,840 lb (9 000 kg), 1,700 mls (2 740 km) with 11,023 lb (5 000 kg), 2,970 mls (4 780 km) with 3,086 lb (1 400 kg); ferry range, 3,075 mls (4 950 km); max. initial climb, 1,705 ft/min (8,67 m/sec); service ceiling, 25,000 ft (7 620 m).

Weights: Empty equipped, 33,950 lb (15 400 kg); normal loaded, 54,013 lb (24 500 kg); max. take-off, 58,422 lb (26 500 kg).

Accommodation: Flight crew of three or four and 44 fully-equipped troops, 32 fully-equipped paratroops or 36 casualty stretchers, two seated wounded and four medical attendants.

Status: First and second prototypes flown on July 18, 1970, and July 22, 1971, respectively, with first production aircraft flying December 23, 1975. One delivered to United Arab Emirates (Dubai) during 1977, together with first two of three for Argentine Army. Italian Air Force committed to procurement of 44 with production of 1·5 per month at beginning of 1978.

AERITALIA G.222

Dimensions: Span, 94 ft 2 in. (28,70 m); length, 74 ft 5½ in (22,70 m); height, 32 ft 1¾ in (9,80 m); wing area, 882·64 sq ft (82,00 m²).

AERMACCHI MB 339

Country of Origin: Italy.
Type: Two-seat basic and advanced trainer.
Power Plant: One 4,000 lb (1 814 kg) Fiat-built Rolls-Royce Viper 632-43 turbojet.
Performance: Max. speed (clean configuration), 558 mph (898 km/h) at sea level, 508 mph (817 km/h) at 30,000 ft (9 145 m) or Mach 0·77; max. range (clean configuration), 1,094 mls (1 760 km), (ferry configuration with two 143 Imp gal/650 l pylon tanks), 1,310 mls (2 110 km); initial climb, 6,600 ft/min (33,5 m/sec); service ceiling, 47,500 ft (14 630 m).
Weights: Empty equipped, 6,883 lb (3 125 kg); loaded (clean), 9,700 lb (4 400 kg); max. take-off, 13,000 lb (5 897 kg).
Armament: For armament training and light strike roles a maximum of 4,000 lb (1 815 kg) may be distributed between six underwing stations, the inner and mid stations being of 750 lb (340 kg) capacity and the outer stations being of 500 lb (230 kg) capacity.
Status: Two prototypes flown on August 12, 1976, and 20 May, 1977, respectively. Six pre-production examples to fly during 1978, of which three to be delivered to Italian Air Force for evaluation, this service having a requirement for up to 100 aircraft.
Notes: Based on the airframe of the earlier MB.326 and incorporating the strengthened structure of the MB.326K, the MB.339 incorporates an entirely redesigned forward fuselage providing vertically staggered seats for pupil and instructor. Photo-reconnaissance equipment or armament pod may be inserted in bay beneath rear seat.

8

AERMACCHI MB 339

Dimensions: Span, 35 ft 7 in (10,86 m); length, 36 ft 0 in (10,97 m); height, 13 ft 1 in (3,99 m); wing area, 207·74 sq ft (19,30 m²).

AERO L 39

Country of Origin: Czechoslovakia.

Type: Tandem two-seat basic-advanced trainer.

Power Plant: One 3,792 lb (1 720 kg) Walter Titan (Ivchenko AI-25TL) turbofan.

Performance: (At 10,075 lb/4 570 kg) Max. speed, 435 mph (700 km/h) at sea level, 485 mph (780 km/h) at 19,685 ft (6 000 m); cruise, 423 mph (680 km/h) at 16,400 ft (5 000 m); max. range (internal fuel and 5% reserve), 528 mls (850 km), (with two 77 Imp gal/350 l drop tanks) 994 mls (1 600 km); initial climb, 4,330 ft/min (22 m/sec); service ceiling, 37,730 ft (11 500 m).

Weights: Empty equipped, 7,341 lb (3 330 kg); normal loaded, 10,075 lb (4 570 kg); max. take-off, 11,618 lb (5 270 kg).

Armament: Four wing hardpoints for max. external ordnance load of 2,425 lb (1 100 kg), typical stores including various combinations of bombs of up to 1,102 lb (500 kg) in weight, pods each containing 16 57-mm rockets, air-to-air missiles or gun pods. A 23-mm cannon may be installed in a faired housing beneath the forward fuselage.

Status: First of five prototypes flown November 4, 1968, and first of 10 pre-production aircraft flown in 1971, series production commencing late 1972. Initial deliveries to Czech and Soviet air forces, and by the beginning of 1978 the L 39 had also been supplied to the air arms of Bulgaria, German Democratic Republic, Hungary and Iraq.

Notes: Adopted as the standard Warsaw Pact basic-advanced trainer (except by Poland), the L 39 forms part of a comprehensive training system, including flight and ground training simulators and mobile automatic test equipment.

AERO L 39

Dimensions: Span, 31 ft 0½ in (9,46 m); length, 40 ft 5 in (12,32 m); height, 15 ft 5⅘ in (4,72 m); wing area, 202·36 sq ft (18,80 m²).

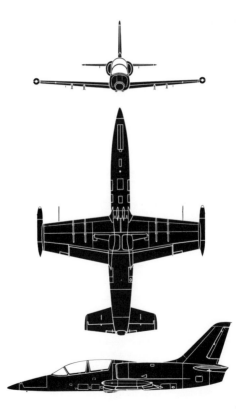

AIRBUS A300B4

Country of Origin: International consortium.

Type: Medium-haul commercial transport.

Power Plant: Two 51,000 lb (23 130 kg) General Electric CF6-50C turbofans.

Performance: Max. cruise, 578 mph (930 km/h) at 28,000 ft (9 185 m); econ. cruise, 540 mph (869 km/h) at 31,000 ft (9 450 m); long-range cruise, 521 mph (839 km/h) at 33,000 ft (10 060 m); range (with max. payload, no reserve), 2,618 mls (4 213 km); max. range (with 48, 350-lb/21 932-kg payload), 3,994 mls (6 428 km).

Weights: Operational empty, 194,130 lb (85 060 kg); max. take-off, 347,200 lb (157 500 kg).

Accommodation: Crew of three on flight deck with provision for two-man operation. Seating for 220–336 passengers in main cabin in six-, seven- or eight-abreast layout.

Status: First and second A300Bs flown October 28, 1972, and February 5, 1973, respectively, with third (to B2 standard) flying on June 28, 1973. First A300B4 flown December 26, 1974. Forty-three had been delivered by beginning of 1978 when production rate was 1·5 per month.

Notes: The A300B is manufactured by a consortium consisting of Aérospatiale (France), Deutsche Airbus (Germany), Hawker Siddeley (UK) and Fokker-VFW (Netherlands). The A300B2 is the basic production version, the A300B4 being a longer-range version with similar capacity and fitted with Krueger leading-edge wing flaps for improved take-off, the A300B2K being essentially a B2 with the Krueger flaps of the B4. The A300B4-FC fitted with a freight door in the forward fuselage is scheduled to fly in first half of 1978.

AIRBUS A300B4

Dimensions: Span, 147 ft $1\frac{1}{4}$ in (44,84 m) : length, 175 ft 11 in (53,62 m) ; height, 54 ft 2 in (16,53 m) ; wing area, 2,799 sq ft (260,00 m²).

AMERICAN JET HUSTLER 400A

County of Origin: USA.

Type: Light business executive transport.

Power Plant: One 850 shp (derated from 1,089 hp) Pratt & Whitney PT6A-41 turboprop and one 718 lb (326 kg) Williams WR19-3-1 turbofan.

Performance: (Estimated with both power components operating) Max. cruise, 435 mph (700 km/h) at 22,000 ft (6 705) m); econ. cruise, 395 mph (636 km/h) at 35,000 ft (10 670 m); range (30 min reserve), 1,500 mls (2 414 km) at max. cruise, 2,030 mls (3 266 km) at econ. cruise; max. climb, 3,100 ft/min (15,75 m/sec).

Weights: Empty equipped, 4,000 lb (1 814 kg); max. take-off, 7,500 lb (3 402 kg).

Accommodation: Pilot and co-pilot/passenger on flight deck and five passengers in main cabin with central aisle.

Status: First prototype (with PT6A-41 only) was expected to fly late 1977, and second (with both engines) scheduled to fly second quarter of 1978. Initial production deliveries scheduled for late 1978/early 1979.

Notes: Two models are being offered, the Hustler 400 with the PT6A-41 turboprop only and the Hustler 400A (to which the above specification applies) which will also have the WR19-3-1 standby turbofan. The wing of the Hustler is of supercritical design and carries full-span Fowler flaps, and lateral control is provided by two spoilers on each outer wing section. The Hustler is to be certificated as a single-engined aircraft, but the rear-mounted turbofan will be certificated for use during the cruise phase of flight.

AMERICAN JET HUSTLER 400A

Dimensions: Span, 32 ft 7½ in (9,95 m); length, 37 ft 11½ in (11,52 m); height, 10 ft 9 in (3,28 m); wing area, 185·21 sq ft (17,21 m²).

ANTONOV AN-32 (CLINE)

Country of Origin: USSR.
Type: Commercial freighter and military tactical transport.
Power Plant: Two 4,190 ehp Ivchenko A1-20M turboprops.
Performance: Max. continuous cruise, 317 mph (510 km/h) at 26,250 ft (8 000 m); range (with 13,215-lb/6 000-kg payload and 45 min reserve), 500 mls (800 km), (max. fuel), 1,370 mls (2 200 km); service ceiling, 31,150 ft (9 500 m).
Weights: Max. take-off, 57,270 lb (26 000 kg).
Accommodation: Flight crew of five and 39 passengers on tip-up seats along fuselage sides, 30 fully-equipped paratroops or 24 casualty stretchers and one medical attendant.
Status: Flown in prototype form late 1976, the An-32 is expected to enter service with both Aeroflot and the Soviet Air Force from 1979–80.
Notes: The An-32 is the latest development in the An-24 (*Coke*) series of transport aircraft and is intended specifically for operation under hot-and-high conditions. Based on the An-26 (*Curl*) and possessing an essentially similar airframe with combined rear-loading ramp/supply drop door, but featuring a 33% increase in available power, the An-32 is capable of operating from unpaved runways and features a 4,400-lb (2 000-kg) capacity electric hoist and a conveyor in the fuselage to assist in the loading of heavy freight. Obvious differences to the An-26 include the overwing engine installation, enlarged ventral fins, upper wing spoilers and dog-tooth wing leading edges.

ANTONOV AN-32 (CLINE)

Dimensions: Span, 95 ft 9½ in (29,20 m); length, 78 ft 1 in (23,80 m); height, 28 ft 1½ in (8,58 m); wing area, 807·1 sq ft (74,98 m²).

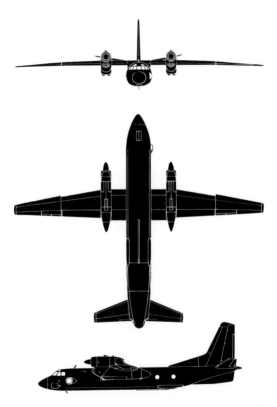

BAC ONE-ELEVEN 475

Country of Origin: United Kingdom.

Type: Short- to medium-range commercial transport.

Power Plant: Two 12,550 lb (5 692 kg) Rolls-Royce Spey 512-14-DW turbofans.

Performance: Max. cruise, 548 mph (882 km/h) at 21,000 ft (6 400 m); econ. cruise, 507 mph (815 km/h) at 25,000 ft (7 620 m); range with reserves for 230 mls (370 km) diversion and 45 min, 2,095 mls (3 370 km), with capacity payload, 1,590 mls (2 560 km).

Weights: Basic operational, 51,814 lb (23 502 kg); max. take-off, 92,000 lb (41 730 kg).

Accommodation: Basic flight crew of two and up to 89 passengers. Typical arrangement provides for 16 first- (four-abreast) and 49 tourist-class (five-abreast) passengers.

Status: Aerodynamic prototype of One-Eleven 475 flown August 27, 1970 followed by first production model on April 5, 1971, with certification and first production deliveries following in June. Total of 222 examples of all versions of the One-Eleven built by beginning of 1978. Co-production agreement for up to 100 aircraft signed with Rumania in May 1977.

Notes: The One-Eleven 475 combines the standard fuselage of the Series 400 with the redesigned wing and uprated engines of the Series 500 (see 1970 edition), coupling these with a low-pressure undercarriage to permit operation from gravel or low-strength sealed runways. The One-Eleven prototype flew on August 20, 1963, production models including the physically similar Series 200 and 300 with 10,330 lb (4 686 kg) Spey 506s and 11,400 lb (5 170 kg) Spey 511s, the Series 400 modified for US operation, and the Series 500 which is similar to the 475 apart from the fuselage and undercarriage.

BAC ONE-ELEVEN 475

Dimensions: Span, 93 ft 6 in (28,50 m); length, 93 ft 6 in (28,50 m); height, 24 ft 6 in (7,47 m); wing area, 1,031 sq ft (95,78 m²).

BAC-AÉROSPATIALE CONCORDE

Countries of Origin: United Kingdom and France.
Type: Long-range supersonic commercial transport.
Power Plant: Four 38,050 lb (17 259 kg) reheat Rolls-Royce/SNECMA Olympus 593 Mk. 602 turbojets.
Performance: Max. cruise, 1,354 mph (2 179 km/h) at 51,300 ft (15 635 m) or Mach 2·05; range with max. fuel (22,250-lb/10 092-kg payload and FAR reserves), 3,915 mls (6 300 km), with max. payload (28,000 lb/12 700 kg) at Mach 0·93 at 30,000 ft (9 145 m), 3,063 mls (4 930 km), at Mach 2·05, 3,869 mls (6 226 km); initial climb rate, 5,000 ft/min (25,4 m/sec); service ceiling (approx.), 60,000 ft (18 300 m).
Weights: Operational empty, 174,750 lb (79 265 kg); max. take-off, 400,000 lb (181 435 kg).
Accommodation: Normal flight crew of three and one-class seating for 128 passengers. Alternative high-density arrangement for 144 passengers.
Status: First and second prototypes flown March 2 and April 9, 1969, respectively. First of two pre-production aircraft flew December 17, 1971, and the first production example following on December 6, 1973, 11 further aircraft having flown by the beginning of 1978 when four more were under construction and scheduled for completion during course of the year.
Notes: The Concorde began to operate its first fare-paying passenger services in January 1976, these being initiated simultaneously by British Airways and Air France which have five and four Concordes respectively. Joint operation of a Concorde service between London and Singapore was initiated by British Airways and Singapore Airlines in December 1977. Preliminary purchase agreements with Iran Air (three) and the Civil Aviation Administration of China (three) had not been firmed-up at the time of closing for press.

BAC-AÉROSPATIALE CONCORDE

Dimensions: Span, 83 ft 10 in (25,56 m); length, 202 ft 3¾ in (61,66 m); height, 37 ft 1 in (11,30 m); wing area, 3,856 sq ft (358,25 m²).

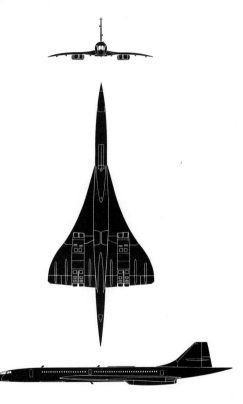

BEECHCRAFT DUCHESS 76

Country of Origin: USA.

Type: Light cabin monoplane.

Power Plant: Two 180 hp Avco Lycoming 0-360-A1G6D six-cylinder horizontally-opposed engines.

Performance: Max. cruise speed, 185 mph (298 km/h); range at max. cruise (with 45 min reserve), 800+ mls (1 290+ km).

Weights: No details available for publication.

Accommodation: Four seats in pairs with dual controls as standard and provision for up to 180 lb (81,6 kg) of baggage in separate compartment.

Status: Prototype flown late summer of 1974 as PD (Preliminary Design) 289 and first production Duchess 76 flown on May 24, 1977. First customer deliveries of the Duchess were scheduled for late that year against orders in excess of 200 aircraft.

Notes: Closely related to the single-engined Beechcraft Sierra 200 and utilising some common structural components, the Duchess 76 is being marketed through Beech Aero Centers (of which there are nearly 100 with more than 4,000 members) at which it is destined to become the primary twin trainer. Intended as a low-cost, high-volume-production aircraft, the Duchess 76 embodies honeycomb-bonded wings, handed propellers, electrically-operated flaps and trim tabs, and, allegedly unique among aircraft in its class, pilot doors in both port and starboard sides, plus a separate door for the baggage compartment.

BEECHCRAFT DUCHESS 76

Dimensions: Span, 38 ft 0 in (11,59 m); length, 29 ft 0 in (8,84 m); height, 8 ft 11 in (2,71 m).

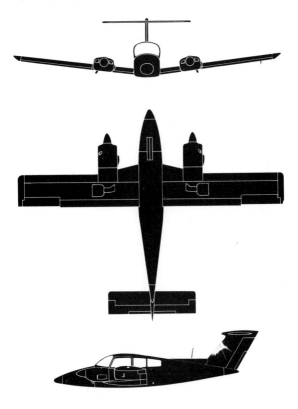

BEECHCRAFT T-34C (TURBINE MENTOR)

Country of Origin: USA.

Type: Tandem two-seat primary trainer.

Power Plant: One 680 shp (derated to 400 shp) Pratt & Whitney (Canada) PT6A-25 turboprop.

Performance: Max. cruise, 213 mph (343 km/h) at sea level, 239 mph (384 km/h) at 10,000 ft (3 050 m); range (5% and 20 min reserve), 787 mls (1 265 km) at 220 mph (354 km/h) at 17,500 ft (5 340 m), 915 mls (1 470 km) at 222 mph (357 km/h) at 25,000 ft (7 625 m); initial climb, 1,430 ft/min (7,27 m/sec).

Weights: Empty equipped, 3,015 lb (1 368 kg); normal loaded, 4,249 lb (1 927 kg).

Status: First of two YT-34Cs flown September 21, 1974, and US Navy contracts for 116 placed by beginning of 1978, with some 80 delivered. Orders placed by beginning of 1978 for 70 examples of T-34C-1 (International) version, including 12 for Morocco, 14 for Ecuador, six for Peru and 16 for Indonesia.

Notes: Updated derivative of Continental 0-470-13-powered Model 45, the T-34C is fitted with a torque-limited PT6A-25 turboprop affording 400 shp, but the T-34C-1 may be fitted with a version of the PT6A-25 derated to 550 shp, wing racks for external ordnance and an armament control system to permit operation as an armament trainer or light counter-insurgency aircraft. With a max. take-off weight of 5,425 lb (2 460 kg), the T-34C-1 has two 600-lb (272-kg) capacity wing inboard stores stations and two 300-lb (136 kg) capacity outboard stations, typical tactical strike ordnance (when flown as single-seater) comprising four 250-lb (113,4-kg) Mk 81 bombs, or two BLU-10/B fire bombs and two SUU-11 gun pods.

BEECHCRAFT T-34C (TURBINE MENTOR)

Dimensions: Span, 33 ft 4¾ in (10,18 m); length, 28 ft 8½ in (8,75 m); height, 9 ft 10⅞ in (3,02 m); wing area, 179·56 sq ft (16,68 m²).

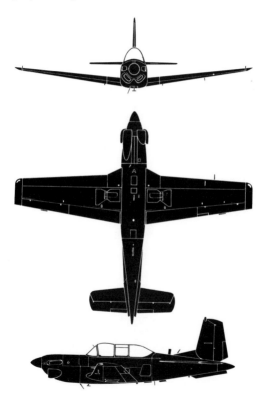

BELLANCA ARIES T-250

Country of Origin: USA.

Type: Light cabin monoplane.

Power Plant: One 250 hp Avco Lycoming 0-540-A4D5 four-cylinder horizontally-opposed engine.

Performance: Max. speed, 215 mph (346 km/h); cruise (75% power), 208 mph (335 km/h), (65% power), 200 mph (322 km/h); initial climb, 1,240 ft/min (6,3 m/sec); service ceiling, 18,100 ft (5 515 m); range (at 55% power with 45 min reserve), 1,170 mls (1 883 km).

Weights: Empty equipped, 1,850 lb (840 kg); max. take-off, 3,150 lb (1 430 kg).

Accommodation: Individual seats for four persons with dual control as standard.

Status: Prototype certificated on July 28, 1976, and initial production batch of 15 scheduled to be assigned to dealers by June 1978, with production planned at 50 per year subsequently.

Notes: The Aries T-250 is the first all-metal aircraft to be produced by the Bellanca Aircraft Corporation, and was initially known as the Anderson-Greenwood T-250, the Anderson-Greenwood company (primarily concerned with the manufacture of industrial valves) having acquired a controlling interest in Bellanca subsequently. Unusual features of the design include an "all-flying" tailplane mounted in "T" position and the use of sprung aileron servo tabs for roll control, the former allegedly providing greater longitudinal stability and more positive control, and the latter being claimed to offer a very high rate of roll.

BELLANCA ARIES T-250

Dimensions: Span, 31 ft 4 in (9,55 m); length, 26 ft 2 in (7,98 m); height, 8 ft 7 in (2,62 m); wing area, 170 sq ft (15,79 m²).

BOEING MODEL 727-200

Country of Origin: USA.

Type: Short- to medium-range commercial transport.

Power Plant: Three 14,500 lb (6 577 kg) Pratt & Whitney JT8D-9 turbofans (with 15,000 lb/6 804 kg JT8D-11s or 15,500 lb/7 030 kg JT8D-15s as options).

Performance: Max. speed, 621 mph (999 km/h) at 20,500 ft (6 250 m); max. cruise, 599 mph (964 km/h) at 24,700 ft (7 530 m); econ. cruise, 570 mph (917 km/h) at 30,000 ft (9 145 m); range with 26,400-lb (11 974-kg) payload and normal reserves, 2,850 mls (4 585 km), with max. payload (41,000 lb/18 597 kg), 1,845 mls (2 970 km).

Weights: Operational empty (basic), 97,525 lb (44 235 kg), (typical), 99,000 lb (44 905 kg); max. take-off, 208,000 lb (94 347 kg).

Accommodation: Crew of three on flight deck and six-abreast seating for 163 passengers in basic arrangement with max. seating for 189 passengers.

Status: First Model 727-100 flown February 9, 1963, with first delivery (to United) following October 29, 1963. Model 727-200 flown July 27, 1967, with first delivery (to Northeast) on December 11, 1967. Deliveries from mid-1972 have been of the so-called "Advanced 727-200" (to which specification refers and illustrations apply) and sales of Model 727s were approaching 1,500 at the beginning of 1978, when 1,320 had been delivered and production tempo was rising from nine to 11 aircraft monthly.

Notes: The Model 727-200 is a "stretched" version of the 727-100 (see 1972 edition). Deliveries of the "Advanced 727" with JT8D-17 engines of 16,000 lb (7 257 kg), permitting an increase of 3,500 lb (1 587 kg) in payload, began (to Mexicana) in June 1974. The 1,282nd Model 727 delivered in August 1977 was Boeing's 3,000th jetliner.

BOEING MODEL 727-200

Dimensions: Span, 108 ft 0 in (32,92 m); length, 153 ft 2 in (46,69 m); height, 34 ft 0 in (10,36 m); wing area, 1,700 sq ft (157,9 m²).

BOEING MODEL 737-200

Country of Origin: USA.

Type: Short-haul commercial transport.

Power Plant: Two 14,500 lb (6 577 kg) Pratt & Whitney JT8D-9 turbofans.

Performance: Max. speed, 586 mph (943 km/h) at 23,500 ft (7 165 m); max. cruise (at 90,000 lb/40 823 kg), 576 mph (927 km/h) at 22,600 ft (6 890 m); econ. cruise, 553 mph (890 km/h) at 30,000 ft (9 145 m); range (max. fuel and reserves), 2,530 mls (4 075 km), (max. payload of 34,790 lb/ 15 780 kg and reserves), 2,370 mls (3 815 km).

Weights: Operational empty, 60,210 lb (27 310 kg); max. take-off, 115,500 lb (52 390 kg).

Accommodation: Flight crew of two and up to 130 passengers in six-abreast seating with alternative arrangement for 115 passengers.

Status: Model 737 initially flown on April 9, 1967, with first deliveries (737-100 to Lufthansa) same year. Stretched 737-200 flown on August 8, 1967, with deliveries (to United) in 1968. Total sales exceeded 550 (including 19 -200s delivered to USAF as T-43A navigational trainers—see 1975 edition) by the beginning of 1978, with more than 480 delivered and production being raised to three monthly by mid-year.

Notes: All aircraft delivered since May 1971 have been completed to the so-called "Advanced 737-200/C/QC" standard embodying improvements in range and short-field performance. Studies were being conducted at the beginning of 1978 for a "stretched" 737-300 using a new wing and "ten-tonne" CFM56 or JT10D engines and having up to 160 seats.

BOEING MODEL 737-200

Dimensions: Span, 93 ft 0 in (28,35 m); length, 100 ft 0 in (30,48 m); height, 37 ft 0 in (11,28 m); wing area, 980 sq ft (91,05 m²).

BOEING MODEL 747-200B

Country of Origin: USA.

Type: Long-range large-capacity commercial transport.

Power Plant: Four 47,000 lb (21 320 kg) Pratt & Whitney JT9D-7W turbofans.

Performance: Max. speed at 600,000 lb (272 155 kg), 608 mph (978 km/h) at 30,000 ft (9 150 m); long-range cruise, 589 mph (948 km/h) at 35,000 ft (10 670 m); range with max. fuel and FAR reserves, 7,080 mls (11 395 km), with 79,618-lb (36 114-kg) payload, 6,620 mls (10 650 km); cruise ceiling, 45,000 ft (13 715 m).

Weights: Operational empty, 361,216 lb (163 844 kg); max. take-off, 775,000 lb (351 540 kg).

Accommodation: Normal flight crew of three and basic accommodation for 66 first-class and 308 economy-class passengers. Alternative layouts for 447 or 490 economy-class passengers nine- and 10-abreast respectively.

Status: First Model 747-100 flown on February 9, 1969, and first commercial services (by Pan American) inaugurated January 22, 1970. The first Model 747-200 (747B), the 88th aircraft off the assembly line, flown October 11, 1970. Some 350 of all versions ordered by 1978, when production was increasing from two to three per month.

Notes: Principal versions are the -100 and -200 series, the latter having greater fuel capacity and increased maximum take-off weight, convertible passenger/cargo and all-cargo versions of the -200 series being designated 747-200C and 747-200F. The first production example of the latter flew on November 30, 1971. Deliveries of the Model 747SR, a short-range version of the 747-100 (to Japan Air Lines), began September 1973. The 747-200B was flown on June 26, 1973 with 51,000 lb (23 133 kg) General Electric CF6-50D engines, and the 52,500 lb (23 810 kg) CF6-50E and the 52,000 lb (23 585 kg) Rolls-Royce RB.211-524 are offered as options.

BOEING MODEL 747-200B

Dimensions: Span, 195 ft 8 in (59,64 m); length, 231 ft 4 in (70,51 m); height, 63 ft 5 in (19,33 m); wing area, 5,685 sq ft (528,15 m²).

BOEING MODEL 747SP

Country of Origin: USA.

Type: Long-haul commercial transport.

Power Plant: Four 46,950 lb (21 296 kg) Pratt & Whitney JT9D-7A turbofans.

Performance: Max. cruise, 594 mph (957 km/h) at 35,000 ft (10 670 m); econ. cruise, 570 mph (918 km/h) at 35,000 ft (10 670 m); long-range cruise, 555 mph (893 km/h); range (with max. payload of 97,080 lb/44 034 kg), 6,620 mls (10 650 km), (with max. fuel and 30,000-lb/13 608-kg payload), 9,570 mls (15 400 km).

Weights: Operational empty, 315,000 lb (140 878 kg); max. take-off, 660,000 lb (299 370 kg).

Accommodation: Flight crew of three and basic accommodation for 28 first-class and 288 economy-class passengers. Max. high-density arrangement for 360 passengers in 10-abreast seating.

Status: First production Model 747SP flown July 4, 1975, with first customer deliveries (to Pan Am) following early 1976. Twenty ordered by beginning of 1978.

Notes: The SP (Special Performance) version of the Model 747 embodies a reduction in overall length of 47 ft 7 in (14,30 m) and retains a 90% commonality of components with the standard Model 747 (see pages 32–33). The Model 747SP is intended primarily for operation over long-range routes where traffic densities are insufficient to support the standard model. Apart from having a shorter fuselage, the Model 747SP has taller vertical tail surfaces with a double-hinged rudder and new trailing-edge flaps.

34

BOEING MODEL 747SP

Dimensions: Span, 195 ft 8 in (59,64 m); length, 184 ft 9 in (56,31 m); height, 65 ft 5 in (19,94 m); wing area, 5,685 sq ft (528,15 m²).

BOEING E-3A

Country of Origin: USA.

Type: Airborne warning and control system aircraft.

Power Plant: Four 21,000 lb (9 525 kg) Pratt & Whitney TF33-PW-100/100A turbofans.

Performance: No details have been released for publication, but max. and econ. cruise speeds are likely to be generally similar to those of the equivalent commercial Model 707-320B (i.e., 627 mph/1 010 km/h and 550 mph/886 km/h respectively). Mission requirement is for 7-hr search at 29,000 ft (8 840 m) at 1,150 mls (1 850 km) from base. Unrefuelled endurance, 11·5 hrs.

Weights: Empty equipped, 170,000 ib (77 110 kg); max. take-off, 325,000 lb (147 418 kg).

Accommodation: Operational crew of 17 comprising flight crew of four, systems maintenance team of four, a battle commander and an air defence operations team of eight.

Status: First of two (EC-137D) development aircraft flown February 9, 1972, one being converted to pre-production standard. Two pre-production aircraft following in 1975, with first production aircraft to USAF on March 24, 1977, six additional aircraft being delivered by beginning of 1978 when 19 of planned procurement of 31 for the USAF approved. Subsequent to 19th aircraft procurement rate of three annually planned. Seven ordered by Iran for delivery from 1979–80.

Notes: E-3A attained operational status late in 1977.

BOEING E-3A

Dimensions: Span, 145 ft 9 in (44,42 m); length, 152 ft 11 in (46,61 m); height, 42 ft 5 in (12,93 m); wing area, 3,050 sq ft (283,4 m²).

BOEING YC-14

Country of Origin: USA.
Type: Medium STOL tactical transport.
Power Plant: Two 51,000 lb (23 154 kg) General Electric CF6-50D turbofans.
Performance: Max. speed, 504 mph (811 km/h) at 30,000 ft (9 150 m), 403 mph (649 km/h) at sea level; range cruise, 449 mph (723 km/h); tactical radius (with 27,000-lb/12 250-kg payload), 460 mls (740 km); ferry range, 3,190 mls (5 130 km); initial climb (at 160,000 lb/72 575 kg), 6,350 ft/min (32,25 m/sec); service ceiling, 45,000 ft (13 715 m).
Weights: Operational empty, 117,500 lb (53 297 kg); max. take-off (STOL), 170,000 lb (77 112 kg), (conventional), 251,000 lb (113 854 kg).
Accommodation: Flight crew of three and max. payload of 62,000 lb (28 123 kg), or six cargo pallets plus 40 troops or max. of 150 troops.
Status: Two prototypes flown August 9 and October 21, 1976. The YC-14 is competing with the McDonnell Douglas YC-15 (see pages 148–149) in USAF advanced military STOL transport (AMST) programme, original programme calling for procurement of 277 examples of selected aircraft.
Notes: The YC-14 is an advanced-technology transport utilising a supercritical wing with full-span variable-camber leading-edge flaps, boundary layer control and USB (Upper Surface Blowing) to achieve a combination of high-speed performance and STOL (Short Take-Off and Landing) performance. USB is provided by engine exhaust gases flowing over the upper wing surfaces and associated flap system. A decision to start engineering development of the YC-14 (or YC-15) was dependent on an assessment of cost-effectiveness against new versions of the C-130 at the beginning of 1978.

BOEING YC-14

Dimensions: Span, 129 ft 0 in (39,32 m); length, 131 ft 8 in (40,13 m); height, 48 ft 4 in (14,73 m); wing area, 1,762 sq ft (163,70 m²).

BRITTEN-NORMAN BN-2A-21
MARITIME DEFENDER

Country of Origin: United Kingdom.

Type: Light maritime patrol and surveillance aircraft.

Power Plant: Two 300 hp Avco Lycoming IO-540-K1B5 six-cylinder horizontally-opposed engines.

Performmances: Max. speed, 180 mph (290 km/h) at sea level; cruise (75% power), 170 mph (274 km/h) at 7,000 ft (2 135 m), (67% power), 168 mph (270 km/h) at 9,000 ft (2 745 m), (59% power), 163 mph (262 km/h) at 13,000 ft (3 960 m); initial climb, 1,130 ft/min (5,82 m/sec); service ceiling, 18,000 ft (5 485 m); endurance (main and tip tanks), 8 hrs.

Weights: Basic empty, 4,012 lb (1 820 kg); max. take-off, 6,600 lb (2 993 kg).

Accommodation: Operational crew (maritime surveillance) of three–four (e.g., pilot, co-pilot, radar operator and camera operator). Up to 10 persons (including pilot) in transport role or 2,240 lb (1 016 kg) of freight.

Status: Introduced in 1977, the Maritime Defender is a version of military variant of the Islander (see 1977 edition) known as Defender, more than 30 of which were included in total sales of 740+ Islanders delivered by beginning of 1978.

Notes: The Maritime Defender is intended to fulfil coastal patrol, fishery surveillance and search-and-rescue roles, and, like the BN-2A-20 Defender, has provision for four standard NATO underwing pylons of 700-lb/317,5-kg (inboard) and 450-lb/204-kg (outboard) capacity for parachute dinghy packs, flares, etc, and Bendix RDR 1300 search radar is installed in the fuselage nose.

BRITTEN-NORMAN BN-2A-21 MARITIME DEFENDER

Dimensions: Span, 53 ft 0 in (16,15 m); length, 36 ft 3¾ in (11,07 m); height, 12 ft 5 in (3,78 m); wing area, 342 sq ft (31,78 m²).

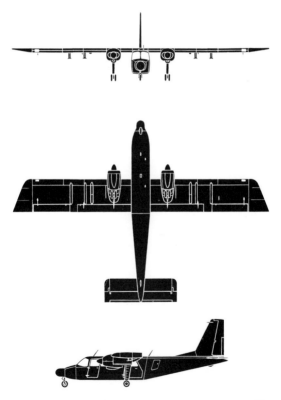

BRITTEN-NORMAN BN-2A MK. III-2 TRISLANDER

Country of Origin: United Kingdom.
Type: Light utility transport and feederliner.
Power Plant: Three 260 hp Avco Lycoming 0-540-E4C5 six-cylinder horizontally-opposed engines.
Performance: Max. speed, 183 mph (294 km/h) at sea level; cruise at 75% power, 176 mph (283 km/h) at 6,500 ft (1 980 m), at 67% power, 175 mph (282 km/h) at 9,000 ft (2 750 m); range with max. payload, 160 mls (257 km) at 170 mph (274 km/h), with 2,400-lb (1 089-kg) payload, 700 mls (1 127 km) at 175 mph (282 km/h).
Weights: Empty equipped, 5,700 lb (2 585 kg); max. take-off, 10,000 lb (4 536 kg).
Accommodation: Flight crew of one or two, and 16–17 passengers in pairs on bench-type seats.
Status: Prototype flown September 11, 1970, with production prototype flying on March 6, 1971. First production Trislander flown April 29, 1971, .and first delivery (to Aurigny) following on June 29, 1971. Trislander production was transferred to Fairey SA at Gosselies, Belgium, late in 1972, and deliveries from the new line began early 1974. Fifty-five Trislanders had been delivered by the beginning of 1978 when future production was uncertain.
Notes: The Trislander is a derivative of the Islander (see pages 40–41) with which it has 75% commonality. The wingtip auxiliary fuel tanks optional on the Islander have been standardised for the Trislander, the extended nose version being known as the Mk. III-2.

BRITTEN-NORMAN BN-2A TRISLANDER

Dimensions: Span, 53 ft 0 in (16,15 m); length, 43 ft 9 in (13,33 m); height, 14 ft 2 in (4,32 m); wing area, 337 sq ft (31,25 m²).

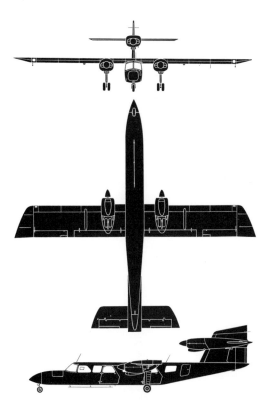

CANADAIR CL-600 CHALLENGER

Country of Origin: Canada.

Type: Light business executive transport.

Power Plant: Two 7,500 lb (3 402 kg) Avco Lycoming ALF 502L turbofans.

Performance: (Estimated) Max. speed, 581 mph (935 km/h), or Mach 0·88; high-speed cruise, 575 mph (925 km/h), or Mach 0·86; normal cruise, 554 mph (891 km/h), or Mach 0·84; long-range cruise, 528 mph (850 km/h), or Mach 0·8; range (at long-range cruise with IFR reserves), 4,623 mls (7 440 km), (at normal cruise), 3,680 mls (5 922 km); time to 41,000 ft (12 495 m), 17 min.

Weights: Empty, 13, 567 lb (6 154 kg); max. take-off, 32,500 lb (14 742 kg).

Accommodation: Basic flight crew of two and typical executive layouts for 10–11 passengers, with commuter configuration for 33 passengers in four-abreast seating.

Status: First of three pre-production aircraft scheduled to fly June 1978, with first customer delivery scheduled for late 1979/early 1980. Production tempo of five per month to be attained by late 1980.

Notes: The Challenger employs a supercritical wing, and freighter and commuter versions are projected.

CANADAIR CL-600 CHALLENGER

Dimensions: Span, 61 ft 10⅕ in (18,85 m); length, 68 ft 6 in (20,88 m); height, 20 ft 5⅛ in (6,23 m); wing area, 450 sq ft (41,80 m²).

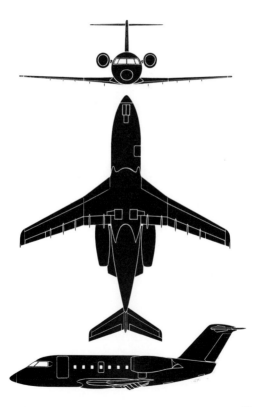

CASA C-101

Country of Origin: Spain.
Type: Two-seat multi-purpose trainer and light tactical aircraft.
Power Plant: One 3,500 lb (1 588 kg) Garrett AiResearch TFE 731-2-25 turbofan.
Performance: Max. speed, 482 mph (775 km/h) at 32,000 ft (9 755 m), or Mach 0·72, 460 mph (740/km/h) at 20,000 ft (6 560 m); max. cruise, 449 mph (722 km/h), or Mach 0·67; range (max. internal fuel), 1,865 mls (3 000 km); ferry range (with external fuel), 2,487 mls (4 000 km); max. climb, 3,350 ft/min (17 m/sec); time to 25,000 ft (7 620 m), 10 min; service ceiling, 45,000 ft (13 715 m).
Weights: Max. take-off (trainer), 10,140 lb (4 600 kg), (ferry), 11,465 lb (5 200 kg), (attack), 12,345 lb (5 600 kg).
Armament: Seven external stores stations with total max. ordnance load of 4,400 lb (1 996 kg).
Status: First and second of four prototypes flown on 29 June and 30 September, 1977, respectively, with third and fourth scheduled to fly first half of 1978. Current planning calling for delivery of first production aircraft against a Spanish Air Force requirement for 60–120 by July 1979.
Notes: The C-101 is being developed with the co-operation of the Northrop Corporation and Messerschmitt-Bölkow-Blohm, and employs modular construction in order to facilitate component interchangeability and maintenance. A lower fuselage bay is available for the installation of a machine gun or cannon, cameras or electronic countermeasures equipment. Operational status with the Spanish Air Force is anticipated in 1980.

CASA C-101

Dimensions: Span, 34 ft 9 in (10,60 m); length, 40 ft $2\frac{1}{2}$ in (12,25 m); height, 14 ft 0 in (4,27 m); wing area, 215 sq ft (19,97 m²).

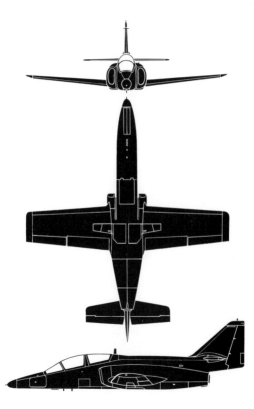

CESSNA 441 CONQUEST

Country of Origin: USA.

Type: Light business executive transport.

Power Plant: Two 625 shp Garrett AiResearch TPE331-8-401S turboprops.

Performance: Max. speed, 338 mph (545 km/h) at 16,000 ft (4 875 m); max. cruise, 332 mph (534 km/h) at 18,000 ft (5 485 m); range cruise, 283 mph (456 km/h); range (with eight passengers and 45 min reserve), 1,595 mls (2 566 km) at max. cruise at 33,000 ft (10 060 m), 1,632 mls (2 626 km) at range cruise at 33,000 ft (10 060 m); initial climb, 2,435 ft/min (12,36 m/sec); service ceiling, 37,000 ft (11 280 m).

Weights: Empty equipped, 5,487 lb (2 489 kg); max. take-off, 9,850 lb (4 468 kg).

Accommodation: Two seats side-by-side on flight deck and maximum of nine passengers in main cabin.

Status: Prototype flown on August 26, 1975, with first customer delivery on September 24, 1977, with more than 40 scheduled for delivery by year's end. Production rate of nine monthly at the beginning of 1978.

Notes: Ceessna's first turboprop-driven business aircraft to attain production status, the Conquest is intended to slot between the company's existing piston-engined twins and the turbofan-powered Citation series. The Conquest's high performance stems in part from use of a new high aspect ratio bonded wing.

CESSNA 441 CONQUEST

Dimensions: Span, 49 ft 4 in (15,04 m); length, 39 ft $0\frac{1}{4}$ in (11,89 m); height, 13 ft $1\frac{3}{4}$ in (4,01 m); wing area, 253·6 sq ft (23,56 m²).

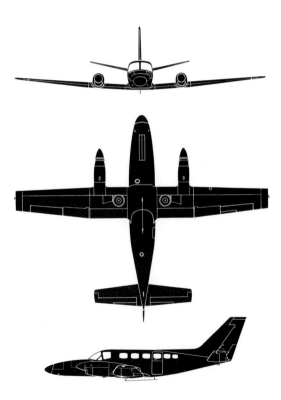

CESSNA CITATION II

Country of Origin: USA.

Type: Light business executive transport.

Power Plant: Two 2,500 lb (1 135 kg) Pratt & Whitney (Canada) JT15D-4 turbofans.

Performance: Max. cruise, 420 mph (676 km/h) at 25,400 ft (7 740 m); range cruise, 380 mph (611 km/h) at 43,000 ft (13 105 m); range (with eight passengers and 45 min reserve), 2,080 mls (3 347 km) at 380 mph (611 km/h); initial climb, 3,500 ft/min (17,8 m/sec); time to 41,000 ft (12 495 m), 34 min; max. cruise altitude, 43,000 ft (13 105 m).

Weights: Typical empty equipped, 6,960 lb (3 160 kg); max. take-off, 12,500 lb (5 675 kg).

Accommodation: Normal flight crew of two on separate flight deck and up to 10 passengers in main cabin.

Status: Two prototypes of Citation II flown January 31 and April 28, 1977, respectively, with first customer deliveries having been scheduled for January 1978, when production comprised five Citation IIs (plus seven Citation Is) monthly, the 400th Citation having been delivered in September 1977.

Notes: The Citation II is a stretched (4 ft/1,22 m longer cabin) version of the original Citation, with a higher aspect ratio wing, uprated engines and increased fuel capacity, and is being manufactured in parallel with the Citation I and I/SP (the latter catering for single-pilot operation) with similar accommodation to the first Citation, JT15D-1A turbofans and a 47 ft 1 in/14,36 m wing. Citation I deliveries began in February 1977.

CESSNA CITATION II

Dimensions: Span, 51 ft 8 in (15,76m); length, 47 ft 3 in (14,41 m); height, 14 ft 11 in (4,55 m).

DASSAULT-BREGUET HU-25A
GUARDIAN (FALCON 20G)

Country of Origin: France.

Type: Medium-range maritime surveillance aircraft.

Power Plant: Two 5,300 lb (2 404 kg) Garrett AiResearch ATF3-6-2C turbofans.

Performance: Max. speed, 540 mph (869 km/h) at 41,000 ft (12 495 m); patrol speed, 240 mph (386 km/h) at 2,000 ft (610 m); range (max. payload and reduced fuel with 45 min reserve), 1,840 mls (2 960 km) at 40,000 ft (12 190 m); max. range (with five crew, full avionics and 45 min reserve), 2,500 mls (4 020 km).

Weights: Empty equipped, 18,705 lb (8 485 kg); max. take-off, 30,500 lb (13 835 kg).

Accommodation: Two pilots with full dual control, a surveillance systems operator and two observers. Provision for radar operator's seat and couch for three passengers.

Status: Prototype of Falcon 20G was flown on November 28, 1977, with first delivery of HU-25A version to US Coast Guard planned for August 1979 against order for 41 aircraft to be delivered subsequently at rate of one per month.

Notes: Derived from the Falcon 20F (see 1974 edition) to meet a US Coast Guard requirement for a medium-range maritime surveillance aircraft to replace the Grumman Albatross amphibian, the HU-25 Guardian (alias Falcon 20G) is intended to fulfil search-and-rescue and marine environmental protection missions, secondary tasks including the surveillance of territorial waters, logistics support, short-range aids to navigation and marine science activities. Existing Falcons can be retrofitted with ATF3-6 turbofans.

DASSAULT-BREGUET HU-25A GUARDIAN (FALCON 20G)

Dimensions: Span, 53 ft 5¾ in (16,30 m); length, 56 ft 2⅞ in (17,14 m); height, 17 ft 0¾ in (5,20 m); wing area, 449·93 sq ft (41,80 m²).

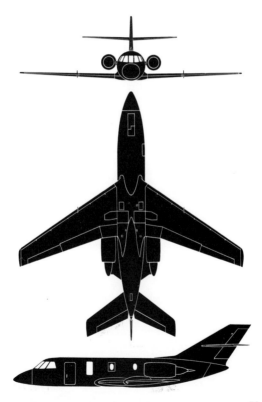

DASSAULT-BREGUET FALCON 50

Country of Origin: France.
Type: Light business executive transport.
Power Plant: Three 3,700 lb (1 680 kg) Garrett AiResearch TFE 731-3 turbofans.
Performance: Max. cruise, 560 mph (900 km/h) at 30,000 ft (9 145 m), or Mach 0·83; long-range cruise, 495 mph (792 km/h) at 37,000 ft (11 275 m), or Mach 0·75; range (with eight passengers and 45 min plus 173-mile/288-km reserve), 3,800 mls (6 115 km) at long-range cruise, 3,454 mls (5 560 km) at 528 mph (850 km/h), or Mach 0·8; max. operating altitude, 41,000 ft (12 500 m).
Weights: Empty equipped, 19,840 lb (9 000 kg); max. take-off, 37,480 lb (17 000 kg).
Accommodation: Flight crew of two and various cabin arrangements for six to ten passengers.
Status: First prototype flown November 7, 1976, with second prototype scheduled to fly February 1978. First delivery of production (unequipped) aircraft set for March 1979.
Notes: Subsequent to initial flight testing, the first prototype Falcon 50 (alias Mystère 50) was modified to incorporate a supercritical wing, which, having the same planform as the original wing, has resulted in significant improvements in speed, range, climb and fuel consumption. An initial production batch of 25 aircraft had been authorised by the beginning of 1978 when it was anticipated that production tempo would build up to three per month during 1980. Flight testing with the supercritical wing was initiated on May 6, 1977.

DASSAULT-BREGUET FALCON 50

Dimensions: Span, 62 ft 2⅝ in (18,96 m); length, 60 ft 9 in (18,52 m); height, 22 ft 10⅝ in (6,97 m); wing area, 504·13 sq ft (46,83 m²).

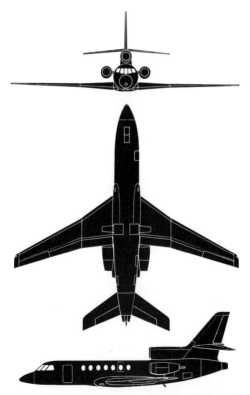

DASSAULT-BREGUET MIRAGE F1

Country of Origin: France.
Type: Single-seat multi-purpose fighter.
Power Plant: One 11,023 lb (5 000 kg) dry and 15,873 lb (7 200 kg) reheat SNECMA Atar 9K-50 turbojet.
Performance: Max. speed (clean), 915 mph (1 472 km/h) or Mach 1·2 at sea level, 1,450 mph (2 335 km/h) or Mach 2·2 at 39,370 ft (12 000 m); range cruise, 550 mph (885 km/h) at 29,530 ft (9 000 m); range with max. external fuel, 2,050 mls (3 300 km), with max. external combat load of 8,818 lb (4 000 kg), 560 mls (900 km), with external combat load of 4,410 lb (2 000 kg), 1,430 mls (2 300 km); service ceiling, 65,600 ft (20 000 m).
Weights: Empty, 16,314 lb (7 400 kg); loaded (clean), 24,030 lb (10 900 kg); max. take-off, 32,850 lb (14 900 kg).
Armament: Two 30-mm DEFA cannon and (intercept) 1-3 Matra 530 Magic and two AIM-9 Sidewinder AAMs.
Status: First of four prototypes flown December 23, 1966. First production for *Armée de l'Air* flown February 15, 1973. Production rate of four–five per month at beginning of 1978. Licence manufacture is being undertaken in South Africa. Firm orders totalled 456 aircraft by beginning of 1978, including Greece, 40 (F1CG), Kuwait, 20 (18 F1CK and two F1BK), Libya, 38 (32 F1ED and six F1BD), Iraq, 36 (inc. four F1B), Morocco, 50 (F1CH), South Africa, 48 (16 F1CZ and 32 F1AZ), Spain, 15 (F1CE), and Ecuador, 18. The total *Armée de l'Air* requirement is 204.
Notes: Production versions currently comprise F1A and F1E for ground attack role, the former for VFR operations only, the F1B tandem two-seat conversion trainer and the F1C interceptor.

DASSAULT-BREGUET MIRAGE F1

Dimensions: Span, 27 ft 6¾ in (8,40 m); length, 49 ft 2½ in (15,00 m); height, 14 ft 9 in (4,50 m); wing area, 269·098 sq ft (25 m²).

DASSAULT-BREGUET MIRAGE 2000

Country of Origin: France.

Type: Single-seat multi-role fighter.

Power Plant: One 18,740 lb (8500 kg) reheat SNECMA M53-2 turbojet. (Production) one 19,840 lb (9000 kg) reheat M53-5 turbojet.

Performance: (Estimated) Max. speed (air superiority version with M53-5), 1,452–1,520 mph (2335–2445 km/h) above 36,090 (11 000 m), or Mach 2·2–2·3; time to Mach 2·0 at 49,200 ft (15 000 m) from brakes release (with two Matra Super 530 and two Matra 550 Magic AAMs), 4 min; tactical radius (with four AAMs and two 374 Imp gal/1 700 l drop tanks), 435 mls (700 km).

Weights: (Estimated) Loaded (intercept configuration with four AAMs), 21,825 lb (9 900 kg), (strike configuration with max. external ordnance load), 33,070 lb (15 000 kg).

Armament: Two 30-mm DEFA cannon and (air superiority) two Matra 550 Magic and two Matra Super 530 air-to-air missiles, or (strike) up to 11,025 lb (5 000 kg) of ordnance on nine external stations (five beneath the fuselage and four beneath the wings).

Status: First of five prototypes scheduled to commence flight testing during first quarter of 1978, with remainder flying 1979–80, the third prototype being a tandem two-seater. Initial contracts anticipated for approx. 130 in "air defence" configuration with deliveries commencing mid-1982, total *Armée de l'Air* requirement for 400 of which half for strike and reconnaissance. Production rate of four per month anticipated by 1984.

Notes: A private-venture twin-M53 derivative, the Super Mirage 4000, is scheduled to fly in the last quarter of 1978.

58

DASSAULT-BREGUET MIRAGE 2000

Dimensions: (Estimated) Span, 29 ft 6 in (9,00 m); length, 50 ft 3½ in (15,33 m); wing area, 430·5 sq ft (40,00 m²).

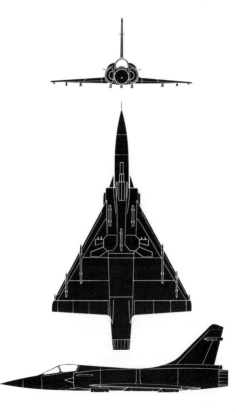

DASSAULT-BREGUET SUPER ÉTENDARD

Country of Origin: France.

Type: Single-seat shipboard strike fighter.

Power Plant: One 11,025 lb (5 000 kg) SNECMA Atar 8K-50 turbojet.

Performance: Max. speed, 745 mph (1 200 km/h) at 985 ft (300 m) or Mach 0·97, 695 mph (1 118 km/h) at 36,000 ft (11 000 m) or Mach 1·05; radius of action (hi-lo-hi with 2,200-lb/998-kg bomb load), 225 mls (360 km), (lo-lo-lo), 160 mls (260 km), (anti-shipping mission with AM-39 Exocet ASM and 1,700-lb/771-kg bomb load), 255 mls (410 km); initial climb, 19,685 ft/min (100 m/sec).

Weights: Empty, 14,220 lb (6 450 kg); max. take-off (catapult), 25,350 lb (11 500 kg); overload, 26,455 lb (12 000 kg).

Armament: Two 30-mm DEFA 552A cannon with 122 rpg and a variety of ordnance on five external stores stations (four wing and one fuselage), including Matra 550 Magic AAMs, AM-39 Exocet ASM, etc.

Status: First of three Super Étendard development aircraft (converted from Étendard airframes) flown on October 28, 1974, the second and third flying on March 28 and March 9, 1975, respectively. First production aircraft built against initial contracts for 50 flown November 24, 1977. Further 21 scheduled to be ordered in FY 1978 and FY 1979 to meet total requirement for 71.

Notes: The Super Etendard is a more powerful derivative of the Étendard IVM (see 1965 edition) with new avionics, a revised wing and other changes. The Super Étendard is intended to serve aboard the carriers *Clémenceau* and *Foch*, and the aircraft is scheduled to enter French Navy service during the course of 1979.

DASSULT-BREGUET SUPER ÉTENDARD

Dimensions: Span, 31 ft 6 in (9,60 m); length, 46 ft 11½ in (14,31 m); height, 12 ft 8 in (3,85 m); wing area, 306·77 sq ft (28,50 m²).

DASSAULT-BREGUET/DORNIER
ALPHA JET

Countries of Origin: France and Federal Germany.
Type: Two-seat basic-advanced trainer and light tactical aircraft.
Power Plant: Two 2,975 lb (1 350 kg) SNECMA-Turboméca Larzac 04-C5 turbofans.
Performance: Max. speed, 616 mph (991 km/h) at 3,280 ft (1 000 m), 560 mph (901 km/h) at 40,000 ft (12 190 m), or Mach 0·85; tactical radius (trainer in clean condition—lo-lo-lo), 273 mls (400 km), (ground attack with max. external load—hi-lo-hi), 391 mls (630 km); initial climb, 11,600 ft/min (59 m/sec)' service ceiling, 45,000 ft (13 700 m).
Weights: Empty equipped, 6,944 lb (3 150 kg); normal take-off (trainer in clean condition), 10,780 lb (4 890 kg), (close support), 13,227 lb (6 000 kg).
Armament: (Alpha Jet E) External gun pod with 30-mm DEFA 533 or (Alpha Jet A) 27-mm Mauser cannon. Four external stores stations. Max. external stores, 4,850 lb (2 200 kg).
Status: First of four prototypes flown October 26, 1973, and first production example (Alpha Jet E-1) flown November 4, 1977, with 19 scheduled to be delivered during 1978.
Notes: The Alpha Jet is being built on two final assembly lines (Toulouse and Munich) and current planning calls for approx. 200 each for the *Armée de l'Air* (Alpha Jet E) for the training role and for the *Luftwaffe* (Alpha Jet A) for the close support role, with first of latter to fly in April 1978. Thirty-three ordered by Belgium (Alpha Jet B) for the training role and five ordered by Togo.

DASSAULT-BREGUET/DORNIER ALPHA JET

Dimensions: Span, 29 ft 11 in (9,11 m); length, 40 ft 3 in (12,29 m); height, 13 ft 9 in (4,19 m); wing area, 188 sq ft (17,50 m²).

DE HAVILLAND CANADA DHC-5D BUFFALO

Country of Origin: Canada.
Type: STOL military tactical transport.
Power Plant: Two 3,133 shp General Electric CT64-820-4 turboprops.
Performance: (At 41,000 lb/18 597 kg) Max. cruise, 288 mph (463 km/h) at 10,000 ft (3 050 m); range with 12,000-lb (5 443-kg) payload, 403 mls (649 km), with 18,000-lb (8 165-kg) payload, 690 mls (1 110 km), with zero payload, 2,038 mls (3 280 km); initial climb, 2,330 ft/min (11,8 m/sec).
Weights: Empty operational, 25,000 lb (11 340 kg); max. take-off (assault mission), 41,000 lb (18 597 kg), (transport STOL), 49,200 lb (22 317 kg).
Accommodation: Flight crew of three and 41 fully-equipped troops or 24 casualty stretchers plus six medical attendants/seated casualties.
Status: First DHC-5D flown August 1, 1975, this being one of initial batch of 19 aircraft built against orders which included three for Zaire, two for Togo, two for Ecuador, four for Kenya and seven for Zambia, all of which were fulfilled during 1976. A further batch of 24 DHC-5Ds was subsequently laid down and deliveries were continuing at the beginning of 1978 against orders from Abu Dhabi (four), Mauritania (two) and Sudan (four).
Notes The DHC-5D embodies uprated engines, minor structural changes and increases in maximum payload and gross weight by comparison with the DHC-5A (see 1972 edition), production of which was phased out in 1972 after completion of 59 aircraft.

64

DE HAVILLAND CANADA DHC-5D BUFFALO

Dimensions: Span, 96 ft 0 in (29,26 m); length, 79 ft 0 in (24,08 m); height, 28 ft 8 in (8,73 m); wing area, 945 sq ft (87,8 m²).

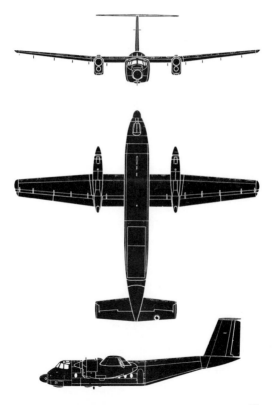

DE HAVILLAND CANADA DASH 7

County of Origin: Canada.

Type: STOL short-haul commercial transport.

Power-Plant: Four 1,120 shp Pratt & Whitney (Canada) PT6A-50 turboprops.

Performance: Max. cruise, 269 mph (434 km/h) at 15,000 ft (4 570 m); long-range cruise, 235 mph (379 km/h) at 20,000 ft (6 560 m); range (with 12,150-lb/5 511-kg payload), 696 mls (1 120 km); max. range, 1,807 mls (2 910 km).

Weights: Empty equipped, 26, 850 lb (12 179 kg); max. take-off, 43,500 lb (19 731 kg).

Accommodation: Flight crew of two and standard seating arrangement for 50 passengers in pairs on each side of central aisle with 300 cu ft (8,49 m³) baggage compartment or 240 cu ft (6,80 m³) compartment and buffet. Various optional passenger/cargo arrangements (e.g., 34 passengers and one pallet, 26 passengers and two pallets or 18 passengers and three pallets.

Status: Two pre-production aircraft flown on March 27 and June 26, 1975. Production commitment for 50 aircraft, of which first flown April 1977, and first customer delivery (second production aircraft to Rocky Mountain) October 1977. First convertible freighter version (fifth production) to be delivered March 1968 (to Wardair). Production rate of one per month scheduled through 1978.

Notes: The Dash 7 received Canadian and US Type Approval during April 1977. A rough field option is being developed with the second prototype and a maritime surveillance version, the Dash 7R Ranger, is in design. A convertible freight version is available as an option.

DE HAVILLAND CANADA DASH 7

Dimensions: Span, 93 ft 0 in (28,35 m); length, 80 ft 7¾ in (24,58 m); height, 26 ft 2 in (7,98 m); wing area, 860 sq ft (79,90 m²).

EMBRAER EMB-110P2 BANDEIRANTE

Country of Origin: Brazil.
Type: Third-level commuter transport.
Power Plant: Two 750 shp Pratt & Whitney (Canada) PT6A-34 turboprops.
Performance: Max. cruise (at 12,500 lb/5 670 kg), 262 mph (422 km/h) at 17,060 ft (5 200 m), (at 10,582 lb/4 800 kg), 267 mph (430 km/h) at 17,060 ft (5 200 m); range cruise, 224 mph (360 km/h); range (max. payload and 30 min reserve), 173 mls (278 km), (max. fuel and 1,307-lb/593-kg payload), 1,191 mls (1 916 km).
Weights: Empty equipped, 7,751 lb (3 416 kg); max. take-off, 12,500 lb (5 670 kg).
Accommodation: Two seats side-by-side on flight deck and 21 passengers in seven rows three abreast in main cabin.
Status: The first EMP-110P2 (146th Bandeirante) flown spring 1977 with production deliveries following during course of year. Production (all versions) three—four monthly at beginning of 1978, with approximately 160 delivered.
Notes: The Bandeirante has been the subject of continuous development since first prototype flew on October 26, 1968, and the EMB-110P2 is one of two stretched and more powerful versions introduced in 1977, the other being the EMB-110K1 military freighter featuring similar engines and fuselage stretch, a reinforced floor and upward-hinging cargo door. It can carry 3,868 lb (1 754 kg) of freight or 19 fully-equipped paratroops. Twenty EMB-110K1s are being delivered to the Brazilian Air Force.

EMBRAER EMB-110P2 BANDEIRANTE

Dimensions: Span, 50 ft $3\frac{1}{8}$ in (15,32 m); length, 49 ft $5\frac{3}{4}$ in (15,08 m); height, 15 ft $6\frac{1}{4}$ in (4,73 m); wing area, 312 sq ft (29,00 m²).

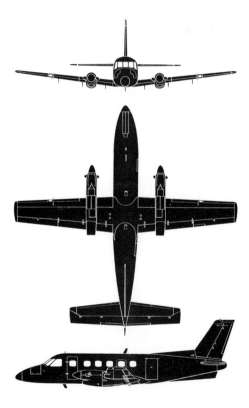

EMBRAER EMB-111M

Country of Origin: Brazil.
Type: Maritime patrol and coastal surveillance aircraft.
Power Plant: Two 750 shp Pratt & Whitney (Canada) PT6A-34 turboprops.
Performance: Max. cruise, 239 mph (385 km/h) at 9,840 ft (3 000 m); patrol speed, 198 mph (318 km/h) at 2,000 ft (610 m); endurance, 8–9 hrs; max. climb rate, 1,190 ft/min (6,04 m/sec); service ceiling, 23,700 ft (7 224 m).
Weights: Max. take-off, 15,432 lb (7 000 kg).
Accommodation: Basic crew of five comprising pilot, co-pilot, radar operator and two observers.
Armament: Provision may be made for six 5-in (12,7-cm) air-to-surface rockets to be carried, these being vertically disposed in pairs on three pylons (two beneath port wing and one beneath starboard).
Status: Sixteen EMB-111Ms ordered in 1976 for the Brazilian Air Force, including two prototypes, the first of which flew in July 1977. Six (EMB-111N) are on order for the Chilean Navy and deliveries to both Brazilian and Chilean services are scheduled for second quarter of 1978.
Notes: The EMB-111 is a derivative of the EMB-110 Bandeirante (see pages 68–69) with a wet wing, which, together with tip tanks, provides a total fuel capacity of 561 Imp gal (2 550 l), AN/APS-128 search radar mounted in a nose randome, provision for a 50-million candlepower searchlight mounted on the port wing, an LN-33 inertial navigation system, a chute for parachute flares and target markers, an eight-person inflatable lifeboat and other sea survival equipment.

EMBRAER EMB-111M

Dimensions: Span (over tip tanks), 52 ft 4¾ in (15,96 m); length, 48 ft 7⅞ in (14,83 m); height, 16 ft 6⅝ in (4,74 m); wing area, 312 sq ft (29,00 m²).

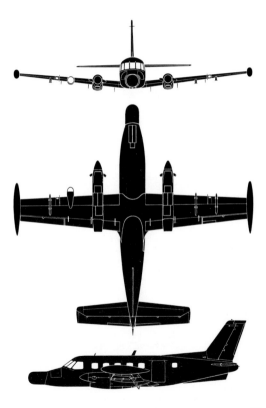

EMBRAER EMB-121 XINGU

Country of Origin: Brazil.
Type: Light business executive transport.
Power Plant: Two 680 shp Pratt & Whitney (Canada) PT6A-28 turboprops.
Performance: Max. cruise, 304 mph (489 km/h) at 12,140 ft (3 700 m); range (six passengers and 45 min reserve), 1,343 mls (2 160 km) at 20,000 ft (6 095 m), (with 1,312-lb/595-kg payload), 1,480 mls (2 383 kg); initial climb, 1,600 ft/min (8,1 m/sec); service ceiling (at 11,464 lb/5 200 kg), 27,300 ft (8 320 m).
Weights: Empty equipped, 7,663 lb (3 476 kg); max. take-off, 12,346 lb (5 600 kg).
Accommodation: Two seats side-by-side on flight deck and individual seats for five–six passengers in main cabin. Alternative high-density configuration for nine passengers three abreast in main cabin.
Status: Prototype flown October 10, 1976, with first production deliveries in third quarter of 1977.
Notes: The Xingu is the first of the EMB-12X series of pressurised light transports evolved from the basic EMB-110 Bandeirante design and utilises the same wing (with reduced span), engine nacelles and undercarriage. At the beginning of 1978, production orders for the Xingu included a small number for the Brazilian Air Force. Further EMB-12X series developments include the 10-passenger EMB-123 Tapajós and the 20-passenger EMB-120 Araguaia which will have essentially similar fuselages to that of the Xingu, incorporating varying degrees of stretch, uprated engines and supercritical wings.

EMBRAER EMB-121 XINGU

Dimensions: Span, 46 ft $1\frac{1}{8}$ in (14,05 m); length, 40 ft $2\frac{1}{4}$ in (12,25 m); height, 15 ft $6\frac{5}{8}$ in (4,74 m); wing area, 296 sq ft (27,50 m²).

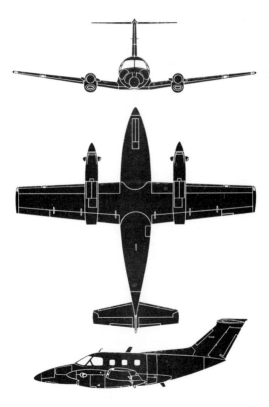

FAIRCHILD A-10A

Country of Origin: USA.
Type: Single-seat close-support aircraft.
Power Plant: Two 9,065 lb (4 112 kg) General Electric TF34-GE-100 turbofans.
Performance: (At 38,136 lb/17 299 kg) Max. speed, 433 mph (697 km/h) at sea level, 448 mph (721 km/h) at 10,000 ft (3 050 m); initial climb, 5,340 ft/min (27,12 m/sec); service ceiling, 34,700 ft (10 575 m); combat radius (with 9,540-lb/ 4 327-kg bomb load and 1,170 lb/531 kg of 30-mm ammunition, including 1·93 hr loiter at 5,000 ft/1 525 m), 288 mls (463 km) at (average) 329 mph (529 km/h) at 25,000–35,000 ft (7 620–10 670 m); ferry range, 2,487 mls (4 002 km).
Weights: Empty, 19,856 lb (9 006 kg); basic operational, 22,844 lb (10 362 kg); max. take-off, 46,786 lb (22 221 kg).
Armament: One seven-barrel 30-mm General Electric GAU-8 Avenger rotary cannon. Eleven external stations for maximum of 9,540 lb (4 327 kg) ordnance (with full internal fuel and 1,170 lb (531 kg) 30-mm ammunition).
Status: First of two prototypes flown May 10, 1972, and first of six pre-production aircraft flown February 15, 1975. First production aircraft flown October 21, 1975, and 339 of planned 733 for USAF ordered by beginning of 1978, when production was five per month with peak rate of 15 per month planned from November 1980. Approximately 75 delivered to USAF by beginning of 1978.

FAIRCHILD A-10A

Dimensions: Span, 57 ft 6 in (17,53 m); length, 53 ft 4 in (16,25 m); height, 14 ft 8 in (4,47 m); wing area, 506 sq ft (47,01 m²).

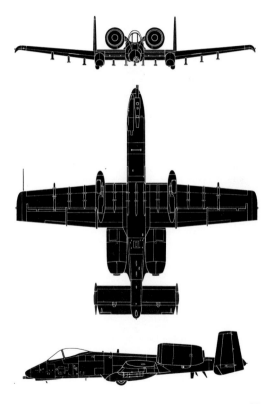

FMA IA 58 PUCARA

Country of Origin: Argentina.
Type: Two-seat light attack and counter-insurgency aircraft.
Power Plant: Two 1,022 ehp Turboméca Astazou XVIG turboprops.
Performance: Max. speed, 311 mph (500 km/h) at 9,840 ft (3 000 m); max. cruise, 298 mph (480 km/h) at 19,685 ft (6 000 m); econ. cruise, 267 mph (430 km/h); range, 870 mls (1 400 km); ferry range, 2,113 mls (3 400 km) at 9,840 ft (3 000 m); initial climb, 3,543 ft/min (18 m/sec); service ceiling, 32,810 ft (10 000m).
Weights: Empty, 8,818 lb (4 000 kg); max. take-off, 14,991 lb (6 800 kg).
Armament: Two 20-mm Hispano HS-804 cannon and four 7,62-mm Browning machine guns, plus max. external ordnance load of 3,570 lb (1 620 kg) distributed between one fuselage and two wing pylons.
Status: First of three prototypes flown on August 20, 1969, and first production aircraft flown on November 8, 1974. Twelve completed by beginning of 1978, when production was proceeding at a rate of 1·5 per month. Further 16–17 aircraft scheduled for delivery during 1978 against total Argentine Air Force requirement for 100 aircraft.
Notes: The Pucará has been designed to meet an Argentine Air Force requirement for a versatile and sturdy aircraft optimised for anti-guerilla operations, using relatively short airstrips and limited maintenance facilities.

FMA IA 58 PUCARA

Dimensions: Span, 47 ft 6¾ in (14,50 m); length, 46 ft 9 in (14,25 m); height, 17 ft 7 in (5,36 m); wing area, 326·1 sq ft (30,30 m²).

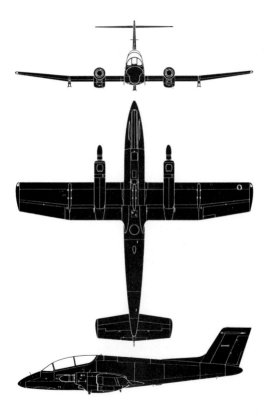

FOKKER F27MPA MARITIME

Country of Origin: Netherlands.

Type: Medium-range maritime patrol and surveillance aircraft.

Power Plant: Two 2,250 eshp Rolls-Royce Dart 536-7R turboprops.

Performance: Cruising speed (at 40,000 lb/18 145 kg), 265 mph (427 km/h) at 20,000 ft (6 095 m); typical search speed, 168 mph (270 km/h) at 2,000 ft (610 m); service ceiling (at 45,000 lb/20 412 kg), 23,000 ft (7 010 m); max. range (cruising at 20,000 ft/6 095 m with 30 min loiter and 5% reserves, with pylon tanks), 2,548 mls (4 100 km); max. endurance, 11 hrs.

Weights: Typical zero fuel, 28,097 lb (12 745 kg); max. takeoff, 44,996 lb (20 410 kg).

Accommodation: Standard accommodation for crew of six comprising pilot, co-pilot, navigator, radar operator and two observers.

Status: Prototype F27 Maritime (converted F27 Mk 100 No. 68) flown on March 25, 1976, and first production aircraft was delivered in the summer of 1977. Initial customer is the Peruvian Navy (2).

Notes: Derivative of Mk 400 transport with Litton AN/APS-503F search radar, Litton LTN-72 long-range inertial navigation system, blister windows adjacent to marine marker launcher and provision for pylon fuel tanks. The Maritime is ostensibly a civil patrol aircraft for off-shore "sovereignty" operations, such as oil-rig and fisheries protection, but has several potential military customers, being suitable for maritime reconnaissance, and is in a similar category to the Hawker Siddeley Coastguarder (see pages 102–103).

FOKKER F27MPA MARITIME

Dimensions: Span, 95 ft 1⅝ in (29,00 m); length, 77 ft 3½ in (23,56 m); height, 28 ft 6⁷⁄₁₀ in; wing area, 753·47 sq ft (70.00 m²).

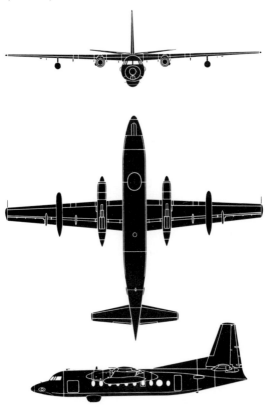

FOKKER F28 FELLOWSHIP MK. 4000

Country of Origin: Netherlands.

Type: Short-haul commercial transport.

Power Plant: Two 9,850 lb (4 468 kg) Rolls-Royce RB.183-2 Spey Mk 555-15H turbofans.

Performance: Max cruise, 523 mph (843 km/h) at 23,000 ft (7 000 m); econ. cruise, 487 mph (783 km/h) at 32,000 ft (9 755 m); range cruise, 421 mph (678 km/h) at 30,000 ft (9 145 m); range (with max. payload), 1,160 mls (1 870 km) at econ. cruise, (with max. fuel), 2,566 mls (4 130 km); max. cruise altitude, 35,000 ft (10 675 m).

Weights: Operational empty (typical), 37,736 lb (17 117 kg); max. take-off, 71,000 lb (32 200 kg).

Accommodation: Flight crew of two and typical single-class configuration for 85 passengers five abreast.

Status: First and second F28 prototypes flown May 9 and August 3, 1967, first delivery following on February 24, 1969. A total of 130 F28s (all versions) had been ordered by beginning of 1978.

Notes: The F28 Mks 1000 and 2000 are now out of production (after completion of 97 and 10 respectively), having been replaced by the Mks. 3000 and 4000, both having unslatted, longer-span wings and Spey Mk. 555–15H engines. The former has the 80 ft 6½ in (24,55 m) fuselage of the Mk. 1000 and the latter has the longer fuselage of the Mk. 2000. Also on offer is the slatted Mk. 6000 (see 1977 edition) with the same high-density accommodation as the Mk. 4000 and having improved field performance and payload/range capabilities. Studies were continuing at the beginning of 1978 for the Super F28 with a new and more advanced wing and accommodation for 115 passengers.

FOKKER F28 FELLOWSHIP MK. 4000

Dimensions: Span, 82 ft 3 in (25,07 m); length 97 ft 1¾ in (29,61 m); height, 27 ft 9½ in (8,47 m); wing area, 850 sq ft (78,97 m²).

GAF NOMAD N24

Country of Origin: Australia.

Type: Light utility transport and feederliner.

Power Plant: Two 400 shp Allison 250-B17B turboprops.

Performance: Max. cruise, 193 mph (311 km/h) at sea level, 196 mph (315 km/h) at 5,000 ft (1 525 m); range cruise, 167 mph (269 km/h); max. range (with 45 min reserve), 985 mls (1 585 km) at 10,000 ft (3 050 m); initial climb, 1,410 ft/min (7,16 m/sec).

Weights: Empty equipped, 4,549 lb (2 063 kg); max. take-off, 8,500 lb (3 865 kg).

Accommodation: Flight crew of one or two and individual seats for 16 passengers. In aeromedical version up to three casualty stretchers and eight seated casualties/medical attendants.

Status: First Nomad N24 (built on production tooling) flown January 1976, and customer deliveries (six to Northern Territory Medical Service) commencing mid-1977 when batch of 25 of N24A version laid down. Approximately 60 Nomads of all versions delivered by beginning of 1978, when production of 120 had been authorised.

Notes: The N24 is a stretched version of the N22B (see 1976 edition) with 24 in (61 cm) increase in nose length and 45 in (1,14 m) increase in cabin length, the N24A having an increased max. take-off weight of 9,400 lb (4 264 kg). Coastal surveillance and patrol variants of the N22B are the Search Master "B" and "L", which, with extended-range fuel tanks, differ in avionics. The Mission Master is a military utility version of the N22B.

GAF NOMAD N24

Dimensions: Span, 54 ft 0 in (16,46 m); length, 47 ft 1 in (14,35 m); height, 18 ft 1½ in (5,52 m); wing area, 324 sq ft (30,10 m²).

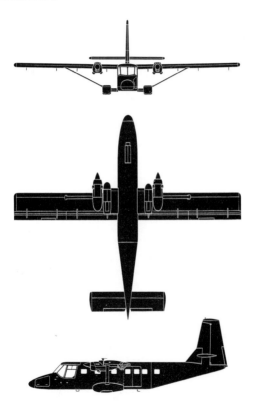

GATES LEARJET 28 LONGHORN

Country of Origin: USA.
Type: Light business executive transport.
Power Plant: Two 2,950 lb (1 340 kg) General Electric CJ610-8A turbojets.
Performance: Max. speed, 550 mph (885 km/h), or Mach 0·81; high-speed cruise, 501 mph (806 km/h) at 41,000–45,000 ft (12 495–13 715 m); econ. cruise, 460 mph (740 km/h) at 49,000–51,000 ft (14 935–15 545 m); max. range (with 1,200-lb/544-kg payload), 1,578 mls (2 540 km).
Weights: Empty equipped, 7,895 lb (3 581 kg); max. take-off, 15,000 lb (6 804 kg).
Accommodation: Two seats side-by-side on flight deck with dual controls and up to six passengers in cabin.
Status: Prototype of Learjet 28/29 flown on August 24, 1977, with first production model scheduled for completion September 1978. The 700th Learjet was delivered on June 15, 1977, and production rate of all models was 10 per month at beginning of 1978.
Notes: The Models 28 and 29 are basically improved versions of the Model 25, deliveries of which commenced in November 1967. The Models 28 and 29 differ in fuel capacity, that of the former being 580 Imp gal (2 637 l) and that of the latter being 654 Imp gal (2 973 l), and utilise the basic Model 25D wing with extended span and Whitcomb winglets of 6 sq ft (0,55 m²) area. The winglets improve cruise, landing characteristics and short-field performance.

GATES LEARJET 28 LONGHORN

Dimensions: Span, 43 ft 9½ in (13,34 m); length, 47 ft 7⅜ in (14,52 m); height, 12 ft 3 in (3,73 m); wing area, 264·5 sq ft (24,57 m²).

GENERAL DYNAMICS F-16

Country of Origin: USA.

Type: Single-seat air combat fighter (F-16A) and two-seat operational trainer (F-16B).

Power Plant: One (approx.) 25,000 lb (11 340 kg) reheat Pratt & Whitney F100-PW-100(3) turbofan.

Performance: Max. speed (with two Sidewinder AAMs), 1,255 mph (2 020 km/h) at 36,000 ft (10 970 m), or Mach 1·95, 915 mph (1 472 km/h) at sea level, or Mach 1·2; tactical radius (interdiction mission hi-lo-hi on internal fuel with six Mk. 82 bombs), 340 mls (550 km); ferry range, 2,300+ mls (3 700+ km); initial climb, 62,000 ft/min (315 m/sec); service ceiling, 52,000 ft (15 850 m).

Weights: Operational empty, 14,567 lb (6 613 kg); loaded (intercept mission with two Sidewinders), 22,785 lb (10 344 kg); max. take-off, 33,000 lb (14 969 kg).

Armament: One 20-mm M61A-1 Vulcan multi-barrel cannon with 515 rounds and max. external ordnance load of 15,200 lb (6 894 kg) with reduced internal fuel or 11,000 lb (4 990 kg) with full internal fuel distributed between nine stations (two wingtip, six underwing and one fuselage).

Status: First of two (YF-16) prototypes flown on January 20, 1974. First of eight pre-production aircraft (six single-seat F-16As and two two-seat F-16Bs) flown December 8, 1976, and first two-seater (fourth aircraft) on August 8, 1977. Final three pre-production aircraft to fly first half of 1978, with first full production F-16A scheduled for delivery August 1978. Current planning call for 1,388 F-16s for USAF (including 204 F-16Bs) and 160 (including 32 F-16Bs) for Iran. Licence manufacture by European consortium for Netherlands (84 plus 18 on option), Belgium (102 plus 14 on option), Denmark (48 plus 10 on option) and Norway (72).

GENERAL DYNAMICS F-16

Dimensions: Span (excluding missiles), 31 ft 0 in (9,45 m); length, 47 ft 7¾ in (14,52 m); height, 16 ft 5¼ in (5,01 m); wing area, 300 sq ft (27,87 m²).

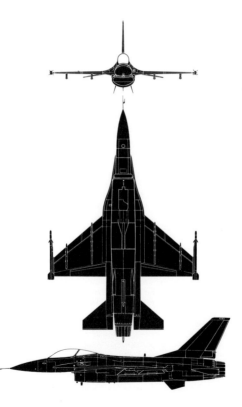

GRUMMAN A-6E INTRUDER

Country of Origin: USA.

Type: Two-seat shipboard low-level strike aircraft.

Power Plant: Two 9,300 lb (4 218 kg) Pratt & Whitney J52-P-8A/B turbojets.

Performance: Max. speed (clean), 654 mph (1 052 km/h) at sea level or Mach 0·86, 625 mph (1 006 km/h) at 36,000 ft (10 970 m) or Mach 0·94, (close support role with 28 Mk. 81 Snakeye bombs), 557 mph (896 km/h) at 5,000 ft (1 525 m); combat range (clean), 2,320 mls (3 733 km) at 482 mph (776 km/h) average at 37,700–44,600 ft (11 500–13 600 m).

Weights: Empty, 25,980 lb (11 795 kg); max. take-off (field), 60,400 lb (27 420 kg), (catapult), 58,600 lb (26 605 kg).

Armament: Five external (one fuselage and four wing) stations each of 3,600 lb (1 635 kg) capacity for up to 15,000 lb (6 804 kg) of stores.

Status: Current production version of the Intruder, the A-6E, first flew on February 27, 1970, and as of September 1975, 66 new A-6Es had been built and 104 modified from A-6A standard. Programme called for last of 94 new-build A-6Es to be delivered in February 1976, but review of requirements led to request for 12 and 15 more in FY 1978 and FY 1979 respectively. Conversion of earlier models to A-6E standard (total of 228) extending through 1979.

Notes: All US Navy and US Marine Corps Intruders are being progressively updated to the latest A-6E standard with TRAM (Target Recognition Attack Multi-sensor) systems, FLIR (Forward-Looking Infra-Red) and CAINS (Carrier Airborne Inertial Navigation System), with fuselage air brakes deleted. The Intruder is also being modified to carry the active-seeker Harpoon missile.

GRUMMAN A-6E INTRUDER

Dimensions: Span, 53 ft 0 in (16,15 m); length, 54 ft 9 in (16,69 m); height, 16 ft 2 in (4,93 m); wing area, 528·9·sq ft (49,14 m²).

GRUMMAN E-2C HAWKEYE

Country of Origin: USA.

Type: Shipboard airborne early warning, surface surveillance and strike control aircraft.

Power Plant: Two 4,910 ehp Allison T56-A-425 turboprops.

Performance: Max. speed (at max. take-off), 348 mph (560 km/h) at 10,000 ft (3 050 m); max. range cruise, 309 mph (498 km/h); max. endurance, 6·1 hrs; mission endurance (at 230 mls/370 km from base), 4·0 hrs; ferry range, 1,604 mls (2 580 km); initial climb, 2,515 ft/min (12,8 m/sec); service ceiling, 30,800 ft (9 390 m).

Weights: Empty, 38,009 lb (17 240 kg); max. take-off, 51,900 lb (23 540 kg).

Accommodation: Crew of five comprising flight crew of two and Airborne Tactical Data System team of three, each at an independent operating station.

Status: First of two E-2C prototypes flown on January 20, 1971, with first production aircraft flying on September 23, 1972. Forty E-2Cs delivered by beginning of Fiscal Year 1978 in which further six to be procured against total US Navy requirement for 77. Four to be supplied to Israel.

Notes: The E-2C is the current production version of the Hawkeye which first flew as an aerodynamic prototype on October 21, 1960. Fifty-nine E-2As were delivered up to 1967 (all subsequently being updated to E-2B standard), development of the E-2C commencing during the following year. All E-2C Hawkeyes delivered subsequent to December 1976 have the new APS-125 advanced radar processing system offering improved overland capability. Israeli Hawkeyes are to have this new equipment.

GRUMMAN E-2C HAWKEYE

Dimensions: Span, 80 ft 7 in (24,56 m); length, 57 ft 7 in
(17,55 m); height, 18 ft 4 in (5,59 m); wing area, 700 sq ft
(65,03 m²).

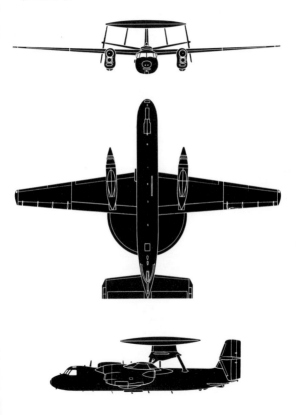

GRUMMAN F-14A TOMCAT

Country of Origin: USA.

Type: Two-seat shipboard multi-purpose fighter.

Power Plant: Two 20,900 lb (9 480 kg) reheat Pratt & Whitney TF30-P-412A turbofans.

Performance: Design max. speed (clean), 1,545 mph (2 486 km/h) at 40,000 ft (12 190 m) or Mach 2·34; max. speed (internal fuel and four AIM-7 missiles at 55,000 lb/24 948 kg), 910 mph (1 470 km/h) at sea level or Mach 1·2; tactical radius (internal fuel and four AIM-7 missiles plus allowance for 2 min combat at 10,000 ft/3 050 m), approx. 450 mls (725 km); time to 60,000 ft (18 290 m) at 55,000 lb (24 948 kg), 2·1 min.

Weights: Empty equipped, 40,070 lb (18 176 kg); normal take-off (internal fuel and four AIM-7 AAMs), 55,000 lb (24 948 kg); max. take-off (ground attack/interdiction), 68,567 lb (31 101 kg).

Armament: One 20-mm M-61A1 rotary cannon and (intercept mission) six AIM-7E/F Sparrow and four AIM-9G/H Sidewinder AAMs or six AIM-54A and two AIM-9G/H AAMs.

Status: First of 12 research and development aircraft flown December 21, 1970, and US Navy plans to acquire a total of 521 with production being completed in Fiscal 1981, procurement currently planned being 44 in FY 1978, 60 in both FY 1979 and 1980, and 42 in FY 1981. Deliveries of 80 to the Iranian Imperial Air Force scheduled for completion mid-1978.

Notes: Studies are continuing of possible higher-thrust engines for the Tomcat as a retrofit programme, candidates at the beginning of 1978 being the 29,000 lb (13 154 kg) General Electric F101X, an uprated version of the Pratt & Whitney F401 and an advanced development of the Allison (Rolls-Royce) TF41 (912-B32).

GRUMMAN F-14A TOMCAT

Dimensions: Span (max.), 64 ft $1\frac{1}{2}$ in (19,55 m), (min.), 37 ft 7 in (11,45 m), (overswept on deck), 33 ft $3\frac{1}{2}$ in (10,15 m); length, 61 ft $11\frac{7}{8}$ in (18,90 m); height, 16 ft 0 in (4,88 m); wing area, 565 sq ft (52,5 m²).

GRUMMAN AMERICAN GA-7 COUGAR

Country of Origin: USA.
Type: Light cabin monoplane.
Power Plant: Two 160 hp Avco Lycoming 0-360-D1D four-cylinder horizontally-opposed engines.
Performance: Max. speed, 200 mph (322 km/h) at sea level; cruise (75% power), 190 mph (306 km/h); max. range (no reserve), 1,265 mls (2 030 km); endurance, 6·8 hrs; initial climb, 1,200 ft/min (6,1 m/sec); service ceiling, 17,500 ft (5 335 m).
Weights: Max. take-off, 3,800 lb (1 724 kg).
Accommodation: Four persons in pairs with space provision for fifth and sixth seats.
Status: Prototype Cougar flown on December 20, 1974, with production prototype following on January 12, 1977. Customer deliveries were expected to commence late 1977.
Notes: Intended to fill a market gap existing between high-performance single-engined light aircraft and current light twins, the Cougar has undergone considerable re-engineering since the début of the initial prototype, the fuselage having been widened, a cabin door replacing a sliding hood, inward rather than outward retraction being adopted for the undercarriage and a wet wing being introduced. Plans exist to develop turbo-supercharged and 180 hp-engined variants of the basic Cougar design, and a 210 hp-engined model is also in prospect.

GRUMMAN AMERICAN GA-7 COUGAR

Dimensions: Span, 36 ft 10½ in (11,23 m); length, 29 ft 10 in (9,10 m); height, 10 ft 4 in (3,16 m); wing area, 184 sq ft (17,10 m²).

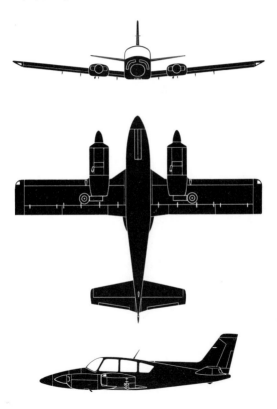

HAL AJEET

Country of Origin: India (UK).
Type: Single-seat lightweight fighter.
Power Plant: One 4,500 lb (2 043 kg) HAL-built Rolls-Royce Bristol Orpheus 701-01 turbojet.
Performance: (Clean configuration) Max. speed, 668 mph (1 075 km/h) at 39,375 ft (12 000 m), or Mach 0·96, 685 mph (1 102 km/h) at sea level; tactical radius (lo-lo-lo with two 30 Imp gal/137 l drop tanks and two Arrow rocket pods), 161 mls (259 km), (with two Arrow pods and two 500-lb/227-kg bombs), 127 mls (204 km); time to 39,375 ft (12 000 m) in clean configuration, 6·03 min; service ceiling, 39,375 ft (12 000 m).
Weights: Basic empty, 5,074 lb (2 302 kg); loaded (clean), 7,803 lb (3 539 kg); max. take-off, 9,195 lb (4 170 kg).
Armament: Two 30-mm Aden cannon with 90 rpg and four wing hardpoints each carrying one Arrow pod containing 18 68-mm rockets, or Arrow pods on outboard hardpoints and a 500-lb (227-kg) bomb on each inboard hardpoint.
Status: First Ajeet prototype (214th HAL-built Gnat modified) flown March 6, 1975, and second (215th Gnat airframe) on November 5, 1975. First production Ajeet flown September 30, 1976, and production of 100 plus for Indian Air Force programmed at beginning of 1978.
Notes: The Ajeet (Unconquerable) is derivative of licence-built Folland (Hawker Siddeley) Gnat from which it differs primarily in having integral wing fuel tankage, zero-level Martin Baker Mk. GF4 (rather than Folland Type 2G) ejection seat, a Ferranti Isis F-195 (in place of GGS Mk. 8) gunsight and upgraded avionics. First of two prototypes of a tandem two-seat trainer version with elevated rear seat and lengthened (by 4 ft 7 in/1,40 m) rear fuselage is scheduled to fly late 1978 or early 1979, with production deliveries of Ajeet Trainer commencing 1981.

HAL AJEET

Dimensions: Span, 22 ft 1 in (6,73 m); length, 29 ft 8 in (9,04 m); height, 8 ft 1 in (2,46 m); wing area, 136·6 sq ft (12,69 m²).

HAL HPT-32

Country of Origin: India.
Type: Side-by-Side two-seat primary-basic trainer.
Power Plant: One 260 hp Avco Lycoming AEIO-540-D4B5 six-cylinder horizontally-opposed engine.
Performance: Max. speed, 154 mph (249 km/h) at sea level, 140 mph (225 km/h) at 4,920 ft (1 500 m), 124 mph (200 km/h) at 9,840 ft (3 000 m); cruise at sea level (75% power), 140 mph (225 km/h), (65% power), 130 mph (210 km/h), (55% power), 121 mph (195 km/h); range (75% power), 540 mls (807 km) at 4,920 ft (1 500 m), (65% power), 505 mls (814 km) at 4,920 ft (1 500 m); initial climb, 1,043 ft/min (5,3 m/sec); service ceiling, 17,390 ft (5 300 km).
Weights: Normal max. take-off, 2,921 lb (1 325 kg).
Status: The first of two prototypes flown January 6, 1977, and current planning calling for the delivery of 100–150 to the Indian Air Force commencing 1980–81.
Notes: The HPT-32 has been designed as a successor to the HT-2 as a primary-cum-basic trainer in Indian Air Force service, and although the prototypes have fixed undercarriages, the trainer has been designed from the outset for a fully retractable undercarriage (this being fixed on the prototypes by introduction of tie rods and exclusion of power control boosters and hydraulic pump). Later production aircraft may switch from the Lycoming to a new 260 hp engine of indigenous design. Provision is made for an optional third seat in the cabin.

HAL HPT-32

Dimensions: Span, 31 ft 2 in (9,50 m); length, 25 ft 4 in (7,72 m); height, 9 ft 7½ in (2,93 m); wing area, 161 sq ft (15,00 m²).

HAWKER SIDDELEY 125 SERIES 700

Country of Origin: United Kingdom.
Type: Light business executive transport.
Power Plant: Two 3,700 lb (1 680 kg) Garrett AiResearch TFE 731-3-1H turbofans.
Performance: High-speed cruise, 495 mph (796 km/h); long-range cruise, 449 mph (722 km/h); range (with 1,200-lb/544-kg payload and 45 min reserve), 2,705 mls (4 355 km); time to 35,000 ft (10 675 m), 19 min; operating altitude, 41,000 ft (12 500 m).
Weights: Typical basic, 13,327 lb (6 045 kg); max. take-off, 24,200 lb (10 977 kg).
Accommodation: Normal flight crew of two and basic lay-out for eight passengers, with alternative layouts for up to 14 passengers.
Status: Series 700 development aircraft flown June 28, 1976, followed by first production aircraft on November 8, 1976. Production of 40 authorised by beginning of 1978, when firm orders exceeded 25 aircraft.
Notes: Series 700 differs from Series 600 (see 1976 edition) that it has supplanted primarily in having turbofans in place of Viper 601 turbojets. Various aerodynamic improvements have also been introduced. Hawker Siddeley was to start converting earlier Viper-engined HS 125s to TFE 731 turbofans from January 1978. The Series 700 was preceded by 72 Series 600 aircraft, 114 Series 400 aircraft and 148 examples of earlier models, plus two prototypes and 20 of a navigational training version (Dominie).

HAWKER SIDDELEY 125 SERIES 700

Dimensions: Span, 47 ft 0 in (14,32 m); length, 50 ft 8½ in (15,46 m); height, 17 ft 7 in (5,37 m); wing area, 353 sq ft (32,80 m²).

HAWKER SIDDELEY 748 COASTGUARDER

Country of Origin: United Kingdom.

Type: Medium-range maritime patrol and surveillance aircraft.

Power Plant: Two 2,280 ehp Rolls-Royce Dart R.Da.7 Mk 535-2 turboprops.

Performance: (Estimated) Max. cruise (at 40,000 lb/18 145 kg), 278 mph (448 km/h) at 15,000 ft (4 570 m); time on station (at mission radius of 230 mls/370 km), 8·5 hrs; endurance (max. internal fuel) 12 (plus) hrs; max. initial climb, 1,320 ft/min (6,7 m/sec); service ceiling, 25,000 ft (7 620 m).

Weights: Empty, 22,827 lb (10 354 kg); basic operational, 26,393 lb (11 971 kg); normal max. take-off, 46,500 lb (21 092 kg).

Accommodation: Basic crew of five comprising two pilots, a tactical navigator and two observer/despatchers. A routine navigator may be accommodated if required. Stores launch area at rear of cabin with launching chute for flares and sea markers.

Status: Prototype conversion of company-owned HS 748 demonstrator flown on February 18, 1977. Basic HS 748 transport being built at rate of 1·5 monthly at beginning of 1978.

Notes: A derivative of the HS 748 Series 2A short- to medium-range transport (see 1976 edition), the Coastguarder is aimed at the growing market for "sovereignty patrol" aircraft, its missions including surface surveillance, off-shore oilfield patrol, fishery protection and search-and-rescue. The Coastguarder features tip-to-tip integral fuel tankage and a ventral MEL Marec search radar, and is also suitable for general maritime reconnaissance where a more sophisticated long-range aircraft is not required. With the extensive introduction of 200-mile (322-km) off-shore exclusive economic zones, it is calculated that a market exists for up to 200 aircraft in the Coastguarder class.

102

HAWKER SIDDELEY 748 COASTGUARDER

Dimensions: Span, 98 ft 6 in (30,02 m); length, 67 ft 0 in (20,42 m); height, 24 ft 10 in (7,57 m); wing area, 810·75 sq ft (75,35 m²).

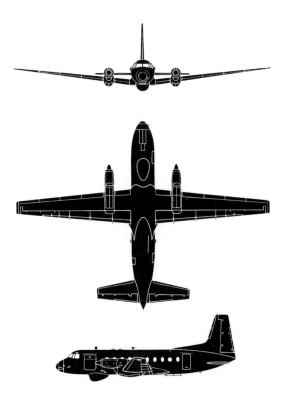

HAWKER SIDDELEY HARRIER G.R. MK. 3

Country of Origin: United Kingdom.
Type: Single-seat V/STOL strike and reconnaissance fighter.
Power Plant: One 21,500 lb (9 760 kg) Rolls-Royce Pegasus 103 vectored-thrust turbofan.
Performance: Max. speed, 720 mph (1 160 km/h) or Mach 0·95 at 1,000 ft (305 m), with typical external ordnance load, 640–660 mph (1 030–1 060 km) or Mach 0·85–0·87 at 1,000 ft (305 m); cruise, 560 mph (900 km/h) or Mach 0·8 at 20,000 ft (6 096 m); tactical radius for hi-lo-hi mission, 260 mls (418 km), with two 100 Imp gal (455 l) external tanks, 400 mls (644 km).
Weights: Empty, 12,400 lb (5 624 kg); max. take-off (VTO), 18,000 lb (8 165 kg); max. take-off (STO), 23,000+ lb (10 433+ kg); approx. max. take-off, 26,000 lb (11 793 kg).
Armament: Provision for two 30-mm Aden cannon with 130 rpg and up to 5,000 lb (2 268 kg) of ordnance.
Status: First of six pre-production aircraft flown August 31, 1966, with first of 77 G.R. Mk. 1s for RAF following December 28, 1967. Production of G.R. Mk. 1s and 13 T. Mk. 2s (see 1969 edition) for RAF completed. Production of 102 Mk. 50s (equivalent to G.R. Mk. 3) and eight Mk. 54 two-seaters (equivalent to T. Mk. 4) for US Marine Corps, and six Mk. 50s and two Mk. 54s ordered (via the USA) by Spain (by which known as Matador), plus follow-on orders for 13 G.R. Mk. 3s and four T Mk. 4s also completed. Production continuing in 1978 with follow-on orders for 24 G.R. Mk. 3s for the RAF, one T. Mk. 4 for the Royal Navy and five Mk. 50s for Spain.
Notes: RAF Harrier G.R. Mk. 1s and T. Mk. 2s converted to G.R. Mk. 1As and T. Mk. 2As by installation of 20,000 lb (9 100 kg) Pegasus 102 have been progressively modified as G.R. Mk. 3s and T. Mk. 4s by installation of Pegasus 103 similar to that installed in Mk. 50 (AV-8A) for USMC.

HAWKER SIDDELEY HARRIER G.R. MK. 3

Dimensions: Span, 25 ft 3 in (7,70 m); length, 45 ft 7¼ in (13,91 m); height, 11 ft 3 in (3,43 m); wing area, 201·1 sq ft (18,68 m²).

HAWKER SIDDELEY HAWK T. MK. 1

Country of Origin: United Kingdom.

Type: Two-seat multi-purpose trainer and light tactical aircraft.

Power Plant: One 5,340 lb (2 422 kg) Rolls-Royce Turboméca RT.172-06-11 Adour 151 turbofan.

Performance: Max. speed, 617 mph (993 km/h) at sea level, 570 mph (917 km/h) at 30,000 ft (9 144 m); range cruise, 405 mph (652 km/h) at 30,000 ft (9 144 m); time to 40,000 ft (12 192 m), 10 min; service ceiling, 44,000 ft (13 410 m).

Weights: Empty, 7,450 lb (3 379 kg); normal take-off (trainer), 10,250 lb (4 649 kg), (weapons trainer), 12,000 lb (5 443 kg); max. take-off, 16,500 lb (7 484 kg).

Armament: (Weapon trainer) One strong point on fuselage centreline and two wing strong points and (ground attack) two additional wing strong points, all stressed for loads up to 1,000 lb (454 kg). Max. external load of 5,000 lb (2 268 kg).

Status: Single pre-production example flown on August 21, 1974, and first and second production examples flown on May 19 and April 22, 1975, respectively. Total of 175 on order for RAF with approximately 30 delivered to that service by 1978 with completion of order scheduled for 1980.

Notes: The Hawk is to be used by the RAF in the basic and advanced flying training and weapons training roles, and both single- and two-seat ground attack versions are being offered for export. The projected single-seat version features more internal fuel, an automatic navigation system and various sensors to enhance weapon delivery.

HAWKER SIDDELEY HAWK T. MK. 1

Dimensions: Span, 30 ft 10 in (9,40 m); length (including probe), 39 ft $2\frac{1}{2}$ in (11,96 m); height, 13 ft 5 in (4,10 m); wing area, 180 sq ft (16,70 m^2).

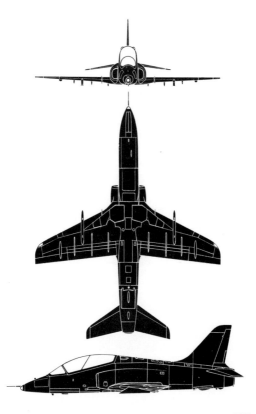

HAWKER SIDDELEY NIMROD M.R. MK. 1

Country of Origin: United Kingdom.
Type: Long-range maritime patrol aircraft.
Power Plant: Four 12,160 lb (5 515 kg) Rolls-Royce RB. 168-20 Spey Mk. 250 turbofans.
Performance: Max. speed, 575 mph (926 km/h); max. transit speed, 547 mph (880 km/h); econ. transit speed, 490 mph (787 km/h); typical ferry range, 5,180–5,755 mls (8 340–9 265 km); typical endurance, 12 hrs.
Weights: Max. take-off, 177,500 lb (80 510 kg); max. overload (eight new-build Mk. 1s), 192,000 lb (87 090 kg).
Armament: Ventral weapons bay accommodating full range of ASW weapons (homing torpedoes, mines, depth charges, etc) plus two underwing pylons on each side for total of four Aérospatiale AS.12 ASMs (or AS.11 training rounds).
Accommodation: Normal operating crew of 12 with two pilots and flight engineer on flight deck and nine navigators and sensor operators in tactical compartment.
Status: First of two Nimrod prototypes employing modified Comet 4C airframes flown May 23, 1967. First of initial batch of 38 production Nimrod M.R. Mk. 1s flown on June 28, 1968. Completion of this batch in August 1972 followed by delivery of three Nimrod R. Mk. 1s for special electronics reconnaissance, and eight more M.R. Mk. 1s ordered in 1973 but retained in storage on completion. Final two of last-mentioned batch to be converted to airborne early warning configuration for service from 1982.
Notes: Total of 11 Nimrod M.R. Mk 1s to be rebuilt for AEW role and remainder being progressively brought up to Mk. 2 standard under a refit programme, changes including new EMI radar, new sonics system, improved navigational system and display system techniques, and increased computer capacity. Refit programme initiated in autumn of 1977.

HAWKER SIDDELEY NIMROD M.R. MK. 1

Dimensions: Span, 114 ft 10 in (35,00 m); length, 126 ft 9 in (38,63 m); height, 29 ft 8½ in (9,01 m); wing area, 2,121 sq ft (197,05 m²).

HAWKER SIDDELEY SEA HARRIER
F.R.S. MK. 1

Country of Origin: United Kingdom.

Type: Single-seat V/STOL shipboard multi-role fighter.

Power Plant: One 21,500 lb (9 760 kg) Rolls-Royce Pegasus 104 vectored-thrust turbofan.

Performance: (Estimated) Max. speed, 720 mph (1 160 km/h) at 1,000 ft (305 m) or Mach 0·95, with typical external stores load, 640–660 mph (1 030–1 060 km/h) or Mach 0·85–0·87; combat air patrol radius (vertical take-off with two 100 Imp gal/455 l drop tanks), 100 mls (160 km) with substantial loiter time.

Weights: Max. take-off (STOL), 25,000 lb (11 339 kg).

Armament: Provision for two (flush-fitting) podded 30-mm Aden cannon with 130 rpg beneath fuselage. Up to 5,000 lb (2 268 kg) of ordnance externally.

Status: First of three development and evaluation Sea Harriers (built on production tooling) is scheduled to fly May–June 1978, with second and third following during second half of year. Total of 24 ordered with deliveries expected to start late 1979 and continue until September 1980.

Notes: The Sea Harrier differs from the Harrier of the RAF and USMC (see pages 104–105) primarily in having a redesigned and raised cockpit, a new nose accommodating Ferranti Blue Fox air–air and air–surface radar, and a revised weapons fit. Provision is made for Sidewinder AAMs on the outboard wing pylons, and the Sea Harrier will lift its max. military load from a 500-ft (152,4-m) flight deck with a 30-knot (55 km/hr) over-deck wind. Comparison should be made with McDonnell Douglas Av-8B (pages 140–141).

HAWKER SIDDELEY SEA HARRIER F.R.S. MK. 1

Dimensions: Span, 25 ft 3 in (7,70 m); length, 47 ft 7 in (14,50 m); height, 12 ft 2 in (3,70 m); wing area, 201·1 sq ft (18,68 m²).

IAI KFIR-C2

Country of Origin: Israel.

Type: Single-seat multi-role fighter.

Power Plant: One 11,870 lb (5 385 kg) dry and 17,900 lb (8 120 kg) Bet-Shemesh-built General Electric J79-GE-17 turbojet.

Performance: (Estimated) Max. speed (50% fuel and two Shafrir AAMs), 850 mph (1 368 km/h) at 1,000 ft (305 m) or Mach 1·12, 1,420 mph (2 285 km/h) above 36,000 ft (10 970 m) or Mach 2·3; max. low-level climb rate, 47,250 ft/min (240 m/sec); max. ceiling, 59,050 ft (18 000 m); radius of action (air superiority mission with two 110 Imp gal/ 500 l drop tanks), 323 mls (520 km), (ground attack mission hi-lo-hi profile), 745 mls (1 200 km).

Weights: Loaded (intercept mission with 50% fuel and two AAMs), 20,700 lb (9 390 kg); max. take-off, 32,190 lb (14 600 kg).

Armament: Two 30-mm DEFA cannon with 125 rpg and (intercept) two or four Rafael Shafrir AAMs, or (ground attack) up to 8,820 lb (4 000 kg) of external ordnance.

Status: Initial production version of Kfir delivered to Israeli air arm from April 1975 with deliveries of improved Kfir-C2 having commenced early in 1977, production rate at the beginning of 1978 reportedly being 2·5 aircraft monthly.

Notes: The Kfir-C2 differs from the initial production Kfir (Young Lion) in having modifications designed primarily to improve combat manœuvrability, these comprising canard auxiliary surfaces which result in a close-coupled canard configuration not unlike that of the Saab Viggen (see pages 190–191), dog-tooth wing leading-edge extensions and nose strakes. Equipped with a dual-mode ranging radar, the Kfir is based on the Mirage 5 airframe.

IAI KFIR-C2

Dimensions: Span, 26 ft 11½ in (8,22 m); length, 51 ft 0¼ in (15,55 m); height, 13 ft 11½ in (4,25 m); wing area (excluding canard and dogtooth), 375·12 sq ft (34,85 m²).

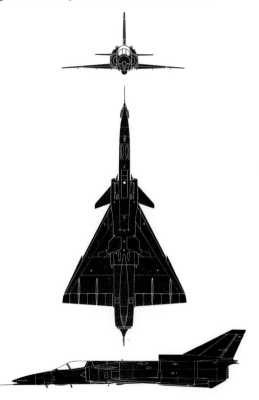

IAI ARAVA 202

County of Origin: Israel.

Type: Light STOL utility transport.

Power Plant: Two 750 shp Pratt & Whitney (Canada) PT6A-36 turboprops.

Performance: Max. speed, 200 mph (322 km/h) at 10,000 ft (3 050 m); max. cruise, 195 mph (314 km/h) at 10,000 ft (3 050 m); range (5,400-lb/2 450-kg payload), 495 mls (796 km), (3,500-lb/1 588-kg payload), 1,036 mls (1 667 km); initial climb, 1,300 ft/min (6,60 m/sec).

Weights: Max. take-off, 16,850 lb (7 643 kg).

Accommodation: Flight crew of one or two and up to 24 fully-equipped troops or 16 paratroops and two despatchers, or 12 casualty stretchers and two attendants in aeromedical arrangement.

Status: Prototype flown early 1977 as development of Arava 201 (see 1976 edition), with production envisaged for 1978–79.

Notes: The Arava 202 differs from the 201 in having Whitcomb winglets, a completely wet wing with single-point pressure refuelling and PT6A-36 engines, which, of similar rating to the -34s of the 201, maintain this at higher temperatures and altitudes. Search and rescue, maritime patrol and surveillance versions are proposed.

IAI ARAVA 202

Dimensions: 69 ft 8 in (21,23 m); length, 42 ft 6 in (12,95 m); height, 17 ft 1 in (5,21 m); wing area (excluding winglets), 470·2 sq ft (43,68 m²).

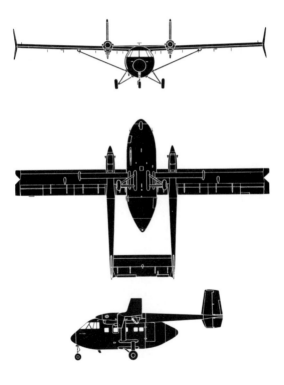

ILYUSHIN IL-38 (MAY)

Country of Origin: USSR.

Type: Long-range maritime patrol aircraft.

Power Plant: Four 4,250 ehp Ivchenko AI-20M turboprops.

Performance: (Estimated) Max. continuous cruise, 400 mph (645 km/h) at 15,000 ft (4 570 m); normal cruise, 370 mph (595 km/h) at 26,250 ft (8 000 m); patrol speed, 250 mph (400 km/h) at 2,000 ft (610 m); max. range, 4,500 mls (7 240 km); loiter endurance, 12 hrs at 2,000 ft (610 m).

Weights: (Estimated) Empty equipped, 80,000 lb (36 287 kg); max. take-off, 140,000 lb (63 500 kg).

Armament: Internal weapons bay for depth bombs, homing torpedoes, etc. Wing hardpoints for external ordnance loads.

Accommodation: Normal flight crew believed to consist of 12 members, of which half are housed by tactical compartment, operating sensors and co-ordinating data flow to surface vessels and other aircraft.

Status: The Il-38 reportedly flew in prototype form during 1967–68, entering service with the Soviet naval air arm early in 1970. Delivery of three for use by Indian Naval Aviation commenced during second half of 1977.

Notes: The Il-38 is a derivative of the Il-18 commercial transport, with essentially similar wings, tail surfaces, engines and undercarriage. By comparison, the wing is positioned further forward on the fuselage for CG reasons.

ILYUSHIN IL-38 (MAY)

Dimensions: Span, 122 ft 9 in (37,40 m); length, 131 ft 0 in (39,92 m); height, 33 ft 4 in (10,17 m); wing area, 1,507 sq ft (140,0 m²).

ILYUSHIN IL-76T (CANDID)

Country of Origin: USSR.
Type: Heavy commercial and military freighter.
Power Plant: Four 26,455 lb (12 000 kg) Soloviev D-30KP turbofans.
Performance: Max. cruise, 497 mph (800 km/h) at 29,530 ft (9 000 m); range cruise, 466 mph (750 km/h) at 39,370 ft (12 000 m); max. range (with reserves), 4,163 mls (6 700 km); range with max. payload (88,185 lb/40 000 kg), 3,107 mls (5 000 km).
Weights: Max. take-off, 374,790 lb (170 000 kg).
Accommodation: Normal flight crew of four with navigator below flight deck in glazed nose. Pressurised hold for containerised and other freight, wheeled and tracked vehicles, etc. Military version has pressurised tail station for sighting 23-mm cannon barbette.
Status: First of four prototypes flown on March 25, 1971, with production deliveries to Soviet Air Force commencing 1974, and to Aeroflot (Il-76T) 1976.
Notes: The Il-76 is being manufactured in both commercial and military versions, the former (Il-76T) being illustrated above and the latter on opposite page. The current production Il-76 has some 20% more fuel capacity than the initial version and a 1,056-mile (1 700-km) range increase, max. take-off weight having been increased by 28,660 lb (13 000 kg). A flight refuelling tanker version of the Il-76 has been developed for the Soviet Air Force, and the aircraft possesses outstanding short-field capability and may be operated from unprepared airstrips, having a multi-wheel undercarriage with variable-pressure tyres.

ILYUSHIN IL-76T (CANDID)

Dimensions: Span, 165 ft $8\frac{1}{3}$ in (50,50 m); length, 152 ft $10\frac{1}{4}$ in (46,59 m); height, 48 ft $5\frac{1}{8}$ in (14,76 m); wing area, 3,229·2 sq ft (300,00 m²).

ILYUSHIN IL-86 (CAMBER)

Country of Origin: USSR.
Type: Medium-haul commercial transport.
Power Plant: Four 28,660 lb (13 000 kg) Kuznetsov NK-86 turbofans.
Performance: Max. cruise, 590 mph (950 km/h) at 29,530 ft (9 000 m); long-range cruise, 559 mph (900 km/h) at 36,090 ft (11 000 m); range (with max. playload—350 passengers), 2,796 mls (4 500 km).
Weights: Max. take-off, 454,150 lb (206 000 kg).
Accommodation: Standard flight crew of three–four and up to 350 passengers in basic nine-abreast seating with two aisles (divided between three cabins accommodating 111, 141 and 98 passengers respectively).
Status: First prototype flown on December 22, 1976, and production prototype flown on October 24, 1977. Service entry (with Aeroflot) is scheduled for 1979, and production is a collaborative effort with Polish WSK-Mielec concern (complete stabiliser, all movable aerodynamic surfaces and engine pylons, and the entire wing will be built in Poland from 1980).
Notes: The first wide-body airliner of Soviet design, the Il-86 has been evolved under the supervision of General Designer G. V. Novozhilov and is intended for use on both domestic and international high-density routes. Four are to be supplied to LOT Polish Airlines in 1979–80 in barter for the initial subcontracts in the IL-86 programme undertaken by WSK-Mielec. A long-haul airliner derived from the Il-86 is expected to undergo flight testing and certification during 1979–81, and it is anticipated that this will be powered by imported General Electric CF6-50 turbofans and will have a full-passenger range of 6,300 miles (10 140 km).

ILYUSHIN IL-86 (CAMBER)

Dimensions: Span, 157 ft 8⅛ in (48,06 m); length, 195 ft 4 in (59,54 m); height, 51 ft 10½ in (15,81 m); wing area, 3,550 sq ft (329,80 m²).

JUROM (IAR 93) ORAO

Countries of Origin: Jugoslavia and Romania.

Type: Single-seat tactical fighter and two-seat operational trainer.

Power Plant: Two 4,000 lb (1 814 kg) Rolls-Royce Viper 632-41 turbojets.

Performance: (Estimated) Max. speed, 700 mph (1 126 km/h) or Mach 0·92 at sea level, 627 mph (1 010 km/h) or Mach 0·95 at 40,000 ft (12 190 m); radius of action with 4,410-lb (2 000-kg) warload (lo-lo-lo), 155 mls (250 km), (hi-lo-hi), 280 mls (450 km); initial climb, 17,700 ft/min (90 m/sec); service ceiling, 44,290 ft (13 500 m).

Weights: (Estimated) Empty equipped, 9,700 lb (4 400 kg); max. take-off, 19,840 lb (9 000 kg).

Armament: Two 30-mm cannon and up to 4,410 lb (2 000 kg) of ordnance on five external stations.

Status: First of three prototypes flown in August 1974. Nine pre-production examples completed during 1976, with first production aircraft against a requirement for some 200 aircraft expected to be delivered during 1978.

Notes: The Orao (Eagle) has been developed jointly by the Jugoslav and Romanian (JuRom) aircraft industries, being designated by the latter as the IAR 93. The Jugoslav SOKO organisation is airframe team leader and is responsible for final assembly from Jugoslav- and Romanian-manufactured components, and the Viper 632 turbojet is licence-manufactured in Romania.

JUROM (IAR 93) ORAO

Dimensions: (Estimated) Span, 24 ft 7 in (7,50 m); length, 42 ft 8 in (13,00 m); height, 12 ft 1½ in (3,70 m); wing area, 193·75 sq ft (18,00 m²).

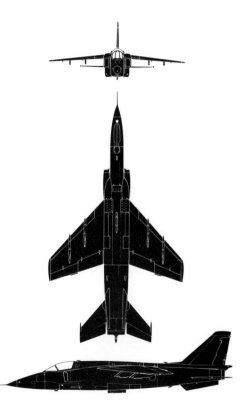

LOCKHEED L-1011-500 TRISTAR

Country of Origin: USA.
Type: Long-haul commercial transport.
Power Plant: Three 48,000 lb (21 772 kg) Rolls-Royce RB.211-524B turbofans.
Performance: (Estimated) Max. cruise, 608 mph (978 km/h) at 31,000 ft (9 450 m); econ. cruise, 567 mph (913 km/h) at 31,000 ft (9 450 m), or Mach 0·84; range (with full passenger payload), 6,053 mls (9 742 km), (with space limited max. payload), 4,855 mls (7 815 km).
Weights: Operational empty, 240,139 lb (108 925 kg); max. take-off, 496,000 lb (224 982 kg).
Accommodation: Basic flight crew of three and mixed-class arrangement for 222 economy (nine-abreast seating) and 24 first (six-abreast seating) class passengers.
Status: First L-1011-500 scheduled to be rolled out on August 23, 1978, and to be flown two months later, with customer deliveries (six to British Airways) to commence mid-1979. Total orders for TriStar (all versions) totalled 167 at beginning of 1978, in which year it is anticipated that 11 will be delivered (as compared with seven in 1977).
Notes: The TriStar 500 is a shorter-fuselage longer-range derivative of the basic L-1011-1 transcontinental version of the TriStar, a 62-in (157,5-cm) section being removed from the fuselage aft of the wing and a 100-in (254-cm) section forward. Versions with the standard fuselage are the L-1011-1, -100 and -200, the last-mentioned model (see 1977 edition) featuring additional centre section fuel tankage and -524 in place of -22B or -22F engines of 42,000 (19 050 kg) and 43,500 lb (19 730 kg) respectively.

LOCKHEED L-1011-500 TRISTAR

Dimensions: Span, 155 ft 4 in (47,34 m); length, 164 ft 2 in (50,04 m); height, 55 ft 4 in (16,87 m); wing area, 3,456 sq ft (320,00 m²).

LOCKHEED C-130H HERCULES

Country of Origin: USA.

Type: Medium- to long-range military transport.

Power Plant: Four 4,050 eshp Allison T56-A-7A turbo-props.

Performance: Max. speed, 384 mph (618 km/h); max. cruise, 368 mph (592 km/h); econ. cruise, 340 mph (547 km/h); range (with max. payload and 5% plus 30 min reserves), 2,450 mls (3 943 km); max. range, 4,770 mls (7 675 km); initial climb, 1,900 ft/min (9,65 m/sec).

Weights: Empty equipped, 72,892 lb (33 063 kg); max. normal take-off, 155,000 lb (70 310 kg); max. overload, 175,000 lb (79 380 kg).

Accommodation: Flight crew of four and max. of 92 fully-equipped troops, 64 paratroops, or 74 casualty stretchers and two medical attendants. As a cargo carrier up to six pre-loaded freight pallets may be carried.

Status: The C-130H is the principal current production version of the Hercules which, in progressively developed forms, has been in continuous production since 1952, and at the beginning of 1978, by which time for the 1,500th Hercules had been delivered (to Gabon), production rate was six per month.

Notes: The C-130H, which was in process of delivery to the USAF, the US Coast Guard, Bolivia, Egypt, the Philippines, Portugal and the Sudan at the beginning of 1978, is basically a C-130E with more powerful engines, and the Hercules C Mk. 1 (C-130K) serving with the RAF differs in having some UK-supplied instruments, avionics and other items. The current production version of the C-130H is known as the "Advanced H" which embodies various refinements.

LOCKHEED C-130H HERCULES

Dimensions: Span, 132 ft 7 in (40,41 m); length, 97 ft 9 in (29,78 m); height, 38 ft 3 in (11,66 m); wing area, 1,745 sq ft (162,12 m²).

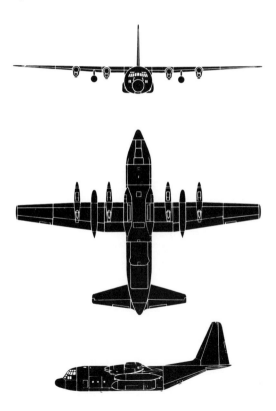

LOCKHEED YC-141B STARLIFTER

Country of Origin: USA.
Type: Heavy military strategic transport.
Power Plant: Four 21,000 lb (9525 kg) Pratt & Whitney TF33-P-7 turbofans.
Performance: Max. cruise, 512 mph (824 km/h) at 38,000 ft (11 590 m), or Mach 0·775; range with max. payload (89,096 lb/44 450 kg), 2,650 mls (4 264 km); max. unrefuelled range (59,800 lb/27 150 kg payload), 4,320 mls (6 950 km).
Weights: Operational empty, 149,904 lb (68 056 kg); max. take-off, 343,000 lb (155 580 kg).
Accommodation: Flight crew of four. Freight hold can accept a total of 13 standard 463L freight pallets totalling 59,800 lb (27 150 kg) in weight.
Status: Sole Y-141B flown on March 24, 1977, and a decision was scheduled for January 1978 concerning conversion of the USAF's current fleet of 271 C-141A StarLifters to similar standard.
Notes: The YC-141B is a stretched version of the original C-141A StarLifter, 285 examples of which had been built when production terminated in 1968. The conversion, which increases cargo capability by 35%, comprises stretching the fuselage (in two sections—ahead and aft of the wing) by 23 ft 4 in (7,12 m) and adding drag-reducing fillets at the leading and trailing edges of the wing roots. In addition, flight refuelling capability is incorporated in a fairing aft of the cockpit above the fuselage pressure shell. The flight test programme with the YC-141B was completed in July 1977, two months ahead of schedule.

LOCKHEED YC-141B STARLIFTER

Dimensions: Span, 159 ft 11 in (48,74 m); length, 168 ft 4 in (51,34 m); height, 39 ft 3 in (11,97 m); wing area, 3,228 sq ft (299,90 m²).

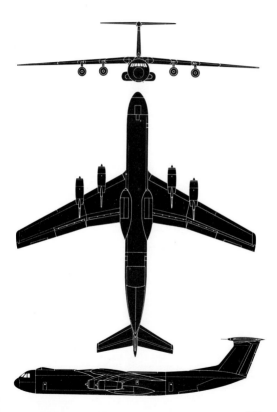

LOCKHEED P-3C ORION

Country of Origin: USA.

Type: Long-range maritime patrol aircraft.

Power Plant: Four 4,910 eshp Allison T56-A-14W turboprops.

Performance: Max. speed at 105,000 lb (47 625 kg), 473 mph (761 km/h) at 15,000 ft (4 570 m); normal cruise, 397 mph (639 km/h) at 25,000 ft (7 620 m); patrol speed, 230 mph (370 km/h) at 1,500 ft (457 m); loiter endurance (all engines) at 1,500 ft (457 m), 12·3 hours, (two engines), 17 hrs; max. mission radius, 2,530 mls (4 075 km), with 3 hrs on station at 1,500 ft (457 m), 1,933 mls (3 110 km); initial climb, 2,880 ft/min (14,6 m/sec).

Weights: Empty, 61,491 lb (27 890 kg); normal max. take-off, 133,500 lb (60 558 kg); max. overload, 142,000 lb (64 410 kg).

Accommodation: Normal flight crew of 10 of which five housed in tactical compartment. Up to 50 combat troops and 4,000 lb (1 814 kg) of equipment for trooping role.

Armament: Weapons bay can house two Mk 101 depth bombs and four Mk 43, 44 or 46 torpedoes, or eight Mk 54 bombs. External ordnance load of up to 13,713 lb (6 220 kg).

Status: YP-3C prototype flown October 8, 1968, P-3C deliveries commencing to US Navy mid-1969 with some 160 delivered by 1978 against planned procurement (through 1982) of 240 aircraft with 14 for delivery in Fiscal 1978.

Notes: The P-3C differs from the P-3A (157 built) and -3B (145 built) primarily in having more advanced sensor equipment. Twelve P-3As have been modified as EP-3Es for the electronic reconnaissance role. Six Orions have been delivered to Iran as P-3Fs, 10 P-3Cs are to be delivered to the RAAF from 1978, and 18 are to be delivered to Canada as CP-140 Auroras from 1980.

LOCKHEED P-3C ORION

Dimensions: Span, 99 ft 8 in (30,37 m); length, 116 ft 10 in (35,61 m); height, 33 ft 8½ in (10,29 m); wing area, 1,300 sq ft (120,77 m²).

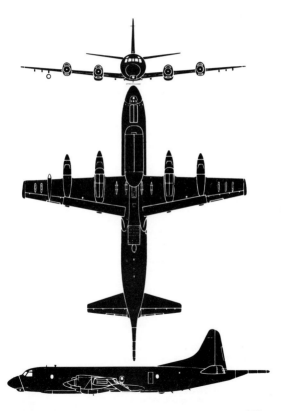

LOCKHEED S-3A VIKING

Country of Origin: USA.

Type: Four-seat shipboard anti-submarine aircraft.

Power Plant: Two 9,280 lb (4 210 kg) General Electric TF34-GE-2 turbofans.

Performance: Max. speed, 506 mph (815 km/h) at sea level; max. cruise, 403 mph (649 km/h); typical loiter speed, 184 mph (257 km/h); max. ferry range, 3,500 mls (5 630 km) plus; initial climb, 3,937 ft/min (20 m/sec); service ceiling, 35,000 ft (10 670 m); sea level endurance, 7·5 hrs at 186 mph (300 km/h).

Weights: Empty equipped, 26,554 lb (12 044 kg); normal take-off, 43,491 lb (19 727 kg); max. launch, 52,539 lb (23 831 kg).

Accommodation: Pilot and co-pilot side by side on flight deck, with tactical co-ordinator and sensor operator in aft cabin. All four crew members provided with zero-zero ejection seats.

Armament: Various combinations of torpedoes, depth charges, bombs and ASMs in internal weapons bay and on underwing pylons.

Status: First of eight development and evaluation aircraft commenced its test programme on January 21, 1972, and remaining seven had flown by early 1973. Current US Navy acquisition of 184 production aircraft to be completed during March 1978, when all jigs and tooling will be retained in place to maintain production capability against follow-on orders.

Notes: Intended as a successor to the S-2 Tracker in US Navy service, the Viking was selected for development mid-1969, and entered fleet service during 1974.

LOCKHEED S-3A VIKING

Dimensions: Span, 68 ft 8 in (20,93 m); length, 53 ft 4 in (16,26 m); height, 22 ft 9 in (6,93 m); wing area, 598 sq ft (55,56 m²).

LTV (VOUGHT) A-7E CORSAIR II

Country of Origin: USA.

Type: Single-seat shipboard tactical fighter.

Power Plant: One 15,000 lb (6 804 kg) Allison TF41-A-2 (Rolls-Royce RB. 168-62 Spey) turbofan.

Performance: Max. speed without external stores, 699 mph (1 125 km/h) or Mach 0·92 at sea level, with 12 250-lb (113,4-kg) bombs, 633 mph (1 020 km/h) or Mach 0·87 at sea level; tactical radius with 12 250-lb (113,4-kg) bombs for hi-lo-hi mission at average cruise of 532 mph (856 km/h) with 1 hr on station, 512 mls (825 km); ferry range on internal fuel, 2,775 mls (4 465 km).

Weights: Empty equipped, 17,569 lb (7 969 kg); max. take-off, 42,000+ lb (19 050+ kg).

Armament: One 20-mm M-61A-1 rotary cannon with 1,000 rounds and (for short-range interdiction) maximum ordnance load of 20,000 lb (9 072 kg).

Status: A-7E first flown November 25, 1968, with production deliveries to US Navy following mid-1969. First 67 delivered with Pratt & Whitney TF30-P-8 (subsequently redesignated A-7Cs). A-7E deliveries approaching 500 at beginning of 1978, with 30 scheduled for delivery during year and final deliveries in 1981.

Notes: A-7E is the shipboard equivalent of the USAF's A-7D (see 1970 edition). Preceded into service by A-7A (199 built) and A-7B (196 built) with 11,350 lb (5 150 kg) TF30-P-6 and 12,200 lb (5 534 kg) TF30-P-8 respectively. Eighty-one early Corsairs (A-7Bs and A-7Cs) under conversion as tandem two-seat TA-7Cs with deliveries continuing in 1978. Delivery of 60 A-7Hs (equivalent to A-7D and illustrated above) to Greece completed in April 1977.

LTV (VOUGHT) A-7E CORSAIR II

Dimensions: Span, 38 ft 8¾ in (11,80 m); length, 46 ft 1½ in (14,06 m); height, 16 ft 0¾ in (4,90 m); wing area, 375 sq ft (34,83 m²).

McDONNELL DOUGLAS DC-9 SERIES 50

Country of Origin: USA.
Type: Short-to-medium-haul commercial transport.
Power Plant: Two 16,000 lb (7 257 kg) Pratt & Whitney JT8D-17 turbofans.
Performance: Max. cruise, 564 mph (907 km/h) at 27,000 ft (8 230 m); econ. cruise, 535 mph (861 km/h) at 33,000 ft (10 060 m); long-range cruise, 509 mph (819 km/h) at 35,000 ft (10 668 m); range with max. payload (33,000 lb/ 14 950 kg), 1,468 mls (2 362 km), with max. fuel (and 21,400-lb/9 700-kg payload), 2,787 mls (4 485 km).
Weights: Operational empty, 65,000 lb (29 484 kg); max. take-off, 120,000 lb (54 430 kg).
Accommodation: Flight crew of two/three and maximum high-density arrangement for 139 passengers in five-abreast seating.
Status: The first DC-9 Series 50 flew on December 17, 1974, with first delivery (against initial order for 10 from Swissair) following during July 1975. Some 65 Series 50 aircraft had been ordered by the beginning of 1978, when total orders for all versions of the DC-9 exceeded 920 aircraft.
Notes: The Series 50 represents a further "stretch" of the basic DC-9 airframe, the fuselage being 6·4 ft (1,95 m) longer than the previously largest DC-9, the Series 40 (see 1972 edition). On October 20, 1977, the decision was announced to proceed with a further "stretched" model as the DC-9 Super 80 to fly in May 1979. The Super 80 is to be powered by 18,500 lb (8 400 kg) JT8D-209 engines, the fuselage is lengthened by 14 ft 3 in (4,34 m) and the wing span and area are increased to 107 ft 10 in (32,86 m) and by 21%, max. take-off weight being 140,000 lb (63 560 kg).

McDONNELL DOUGLAS DC-9 SERIES 50

Dimensions: Span, 93 ft 5 in (28,47 m); length, 132 ft 0 in (40,23 m); height, 27 ft 6 in (8,38 m); wing area, 1,000·7 sq ft (92,97 m²).

McDONNELL DOUGLAS DC-10 SERIES 30

Country of Origin: USA.

Type: Medium-range commercial transport.

Power Plant: Three 52,500 lb (23 814 kg) General Electric CF6-50C1 turbofans.

Performance: Max. cruise (at 400,000 lb/181 440 kg), 594 mph (956 km/h) at 31,000 ft (9 450 m); long-range cruise, 540 mph (870 km/h) at 31,000 ft (9 450 m); range (with max. payload), 6,195 mls (9 970 km) at 575 mph (925 km/h) at 31,000 ft (9 450 m); max. range, 7,400 mls (11 910 km) at 540 mph (870 km/h).

Weights: Operational empty, 261,459 lb (118 597 kg); max. take-off, 572,000 lb (259 457 kg).

Accommodation: Flight crew of three plus provision on flight deck for two supernumerary crew. Typical mixed-class accommodation for 225–270 passengers. Max. authorised passenger accommodation, 380 (plus crew of 11).

Status: First DC-10 (Series 10) flown August 29, 1970, with first Series 30 (46th DC-10 built) flying June 21, 1972, being preceded on February 28, 1972, by first Series 40. Orders exceeded 280 by beginning of 1978 when production was two per month.

Notes: The DC-10 Series 30 and 40 have identical fuselages to the DC-10 Series 10 (see 1972 edition), but whereas the last-mentioned version is a domestic model, the Series 30 and 40 are intercontinental models and differ in power plant, weights and wing details, and in the use of three main undercarriage units, the third (a twin-wheel unit) being mounted on the fuselage centreline. The Series 40 has 53,000 lb (24 040 kg) Pratt & Whitney JT9D-59A turbofans but is otherwise similar to the Series 40.

McDONNELL DOUGLAS DC-10 SERIES 30

Dimensions: Span, 165 ft 4 in (50,42 m); length, 181 ft 4¾ in (55,29 m); height, 58 ft 0 in (17,68 m); wing area, 3,921·4 sq ft (364,3 m²).

McDONNELL DOUGLAS AV-8B

Country of Origin: USA.

Type: Single-seat V/STOL strike and reconnaissance fighter.

Power Plant: One 21,500 lb (9 760 kg) Rolls-Royce F402-RR-402 vectored-thrust turbofan.

Performance: (Estimated) Max. speed, 720 mph (1 160 km/h) at 1,000 ft (305 m), or Mach 0·95, (with typical external ordnance), 640 mph (1 030 km/h) at 1,000 ft (305 m), or Mach 0·85; VTO radius (with 1,800-lb/817-kg payload), 230 mls (370 km); STO radius (with 6,000-lb/2 724-kg payload), 460 mls (740 km), (with 2,000-lb/908-kg payload), 920 mls (1 480 km); ferry range, 2,966 mls (4 774 km).

Weights: Operational empty, 12,400 lb (5 265 kg); max. vertical take-off, 18,850 lb (8 558 kg); max. short take-off, 27,950 lb (12 690 kg); max. take-off, 29,550 lb (13 416 kg).

Armament: Two 30-mm cannon in detachable ventral pod as alternative to centreline stores pylon. Seven external pylons (one fuselage and six wing) with combined capacity of 8,000 lb (3 632 kg).

Status: First of two YAV-8Bs (converted from AV-8A Harrier airframes) scheduled to fly December 1978. Planning at beginning of 1978 called for construction of four development AV-8Bs for trials in 1980–81. US Marine Corps has a requirement for 336 AV-8Bs with service introduction 1984–85.

Notes: The AV-8B is a derivative of the Harrier alias AV-8A (see pages 104–105) with a new and more advanced wing with a supercritical section, largely composite construction and incorporating six hardpoints, redesigned air intakes, various lift improvement devices and new avionics.

McDONNELL DOUGLAS AV-8B

Dimensions: Span, 30 ft 4 in (9,25 m); length, 42 ft 10 in (13,08 m); height, 11 ft 3 in (3,43 m); wing area, 230 sq ft (21,37 m²).

McDONNELL DOUGLAS F-4E PHANTOM

Country of Origin: USA.
Type: Two-seat interceptor and tactical strike fighter.
Power Plant: Two 11,870 lb (5 385 kg) dry and 17,900 lb (8 120 kg) reheat General Electric J79-GE-17 turbojets.
Performance: Max. speed without external stores, 910 mph (1 464 km/h) or Mach 1·2 at 1,000 ft (305 m), 1,500 mph (2 414 km/h) or Mach 2·27 at 40,000 ft (12 190 m); tactical radius (with four Sparrow III and four Sidewinder AAMs), 140 mls (225 km), (plus one 500 Imp gal/2 273 l auxiliary tank), 196 mls (315 km), (hi-lo-hi mission profile with four 1,000-lb/453,6-kg bombs, four AAMs, and one 500 Imp gal/2 273 l and two 308 Imp gal/1,400 l tanks), 656 mls (1 056 km); max. ferry range, 2,300 mls (3 700 km) at 575 mph (925 km/h).
Weights: Empty equipped, 30,425 lb (13 801 kg); loaded (with four Sparrow IIIs), 51,810 lb (21 500 kg), (plus four Sidewinders and max. external fuel), 58,000 lb (26 308 kg); max. overload, 60,630 lb (27 502 kg).
Armament: One 20-mm M-61A1 rotary cannon and (intercept) four or six AIM-7E plus four AIM-9D AAMs, or (attack) up to 16,000 lb (7 257 kg) of external stores.
Status: First F-4E flown June 1967, and production continuing at beginning of 1978. More than 4,900 Phantoms (all versions) delivered by beginning of 1978, with 5,000th scheduled for mid-year delivery.
Notes: Current production models of the Phantom in addition to the F-4E are the RF-4E (see 1972 edition) and the F-4EJ for Japan. The F-4F for Federal Germany, optimised for the intercept role with simplified avionics, entered service with the Luftwaffe from January 1, 1974, and features leading-edge slats and various weight-saving features, the slats now being standardised by the F-4E. The last of 175 F-4Fs was delivered to the Luftwaffe in April 1976.

McDONNELL DOUGLAS F-4E PHANTOM

Dimensions: Span, 38 ft 4¾ in (11,70 m); length, 62 ft 10½ in (19,20 m); height, 16 ft 3⅓ in (4,96 m); wing area, 530 sq ft (49,2 m²).

McDONNELL DOUGLAS F-15 EAGLE

Country of Origin: USA.

Type: Single-seat air superiority fighter (F-15A) and two-seat operational trainer (TF-15A).

Power Plant: Two (approx.) 25,000 lb (11 340 kg) reheat Pratt & Whitney F100-PW-100 turbofans.

Performance: Max. speed, 915 mph (1 472 km/h) at sea level or Mach 1·2, 1,650 mph (2 655 km/h) at 36,090 ft (11 000 m) or Mach 2·5; tactical radius (combat air patrol), up to 1,120 mls (1 800 km); ferry range, 2,980 mls (4 800 km), (with Fast Pack auxiliary tanks), 3,450 mls (5 560 km).

Weights: Empty equipped, 26,147 lb (11 860 kg); loaded (clean), 38,250 lb (17 350 kg); max. take-off (intercept mission), 40,000 lb (18 145 kg); max. take-off, 54,123 lb (24 550 kg).

Armament: One 20-mm M-61A-1 rotary cannon with 950 rounds and (intercept mission) four AIM-9L Sidewinder and four AIM-7F Sparrow AAMs. Five stores stations (four wing and one fuselage) can lift up to 15,000 lb (6 804 kg) of ordnance.

Status: Twenty test and development aircraft ordered (18 F-15As and two TF-15As) with first F-15A flying on July 27, 1972, and first TF-15A on July 7, 1973. Current planning calls for acquisition of 729 Eagles by USAF, every seventh aircraft being a TF-15A, and some 250 aircraft had been delivered by January 1978, when production rate was rising to 11 per month.

Notes: The Eagle is to equip 19 USAF squadrons, deliveries of 25 to Israel commenced on December 10, 1976, and the Eagle has been selected by Japan's Air Self-Defence Force and the Royal Saudi Air Force.

McDONNELL DOUGLAS F-15 EAGLE

Dimensions: Span, 42 ft 9¾ in (13,05 m); length, 63 ft 9 in (19,43 m); height, 18 ft 5½ in (5,63 m); wing area, 608 sq ft (56,50 m²).

McDONNELL DOUGLAS/NORTHROP
F-18 HORNET

Country of Origin: USA.

Type: Single-seat shipboard air superiority fighter.

Power Plant: Two (approx) 10,600 lb (4 810 kg) dry and 16,000 lb (7 260 kg) reheat General Electric F404-GE-400 turbofans.

Performance: (Estimated) Max. speed, 1,190 mph (1 915 km/h) at 36,000 ft (10 970 m), or Mach 1·8; combat radius (internal fuel—escort mission), 480 mls (770 km); ferry range, 2,300+ mls (3 700+ km); combat ceiling, 50,000 ft (15 240 m).

Weights; (Approx.) Loaded (fighter escort mission), 33,580 lb (15 230 kg); max. take-off, 44,000 lb (19 960 kg).

Armament: One 20-mm M-61 six-barrel cannon with 540 rounds and up to 13,700 lb (6 215 kg) of external ordnance on nine stations (two wingtip, four wing and three fuselage), including mix of AIM-7F Sparrow (outboard wing pylons and two fuselage stations) and AIM-9 Sidewinder (wingtips) air-to-air missiles.

Status: First of 11 development aircraft scheduled to fly in September 1978, with second and third in November 1978 and March 1979 respectively, and remainder following at a rate of one per month thereafter. Procurement by US Navy scheduled to commence in Fiscal 1980.

Notes: Intended for US Navy service in the air defence (F-18) and attack (A-18) roles, the Hornet is a derivative of the Northrop YF-17 (see 1975 edition) which is being developed by McDonnell Douglas (as prime contractor) and Northrop.

McDONNELL DOUGLAS/NORTHROP F-18 HORNET

Dimensions: Span, 37 ft 6 in (11,43 m); length, 56 ft 0 in (17,07 m); height, 15 ft 3⅜ in (4,66 m); wing area, 400 sq ft (37,16 m²).

McDONNELL DOUGLAS YC-15

Country of Origin: USA.

Type: Medium STOL tactical transport.

Power Plant: Four 16,000 lb (7 258 kg) Pratt & Whitney JT8D-17 turbofans.

Performance: Max. speed, 403 mph (649 km/h); tactical radius (with 27,000-lb/12 247-kg payload), 460 mls (740 km); ferry range, 2,992 mls (4 814 km).

Weights: Max. take-off weight, 216,680 lb (98 286 kg).

Accommodation: Flight crew of three. Hold can accommodate all US Army vehicles up to and including the 62,000-lb (28 123-kg) extended-barrel self-propelled 8-in (20,3-cm) howitzer. Approximately 150 fully-equipped troops may be carried.

Status: Two prototypes flown on August 26 and December 5, 1975, and the YC-15 is competing with the Boeing YC-14 (see pages 38–39) in USAF advanced military STOL transport (AMST) programme which originally called for procurement of 277 examples of selected aircraft. Development continuing at beginning of 1978 as low-priority programme.

Notes: The first and second prototypes have been respectively employed to test the GE/SNECMA CFM56 and P&W JT8D-209 engines, which in each case replaced a JT8D-17. The first prototype has also been fitted with a 22 ft (6,70 m) longer-span wing as a result of upgrading of the AMST specification after the YC-15 design had been frozen. The YC-15 derives STOL characteristics from a variety of high-lift devices, including double-slotted flaps over some 75% of the wing span and operating in the exhaust stream.

McDONNELL DOUGLAS YC-15

Dimensions: Span, 110 ft 4 in (33,64 m); length, 124 ft 3 in (37,90 m); height, 43 ft 4 in (13,20 m); wing area, 1,740 sq ft (161,65 m²).

MIKOYAN MIG-21BIS (FISHBED-N)

Country of Origin: USSR.

Type: Single-seat multi-role fighter.

Power Plant: One 16,535 lb (7 500 kg) reheat Tumansky R-25 turbojet.

Performance: (Estimated) Max. speed, 808 mph (1 300 km/h) at 1,000 ft (305 m), or Mach 1·06, 1,386 mph (2 230 km/h) above 36,090 ft (11 000 m), or Mach 2·1; tactical radius (intercept mission with centreline drop tank and four K-13A AAMs), 350 mls (560 km); ferry range (max. external fuel), 1,120 mls (1 800 km).

Weights: Approx. normal take-offs (two K-13A missiles and two 108 Imp gal/490 l drop tanks), 20,000 lb (9 070 kg).

Armament: One twin-barrel 23-mm GSh-23 cannon and up to four air-to-air missiles on wing pylons for intercept role. Various external stores for ground attack, including UV-16-57 or UV-32-57 pods containing 16 and 32 55-mm S-5 rockets respectively, 240-mm S-24 rockets or 550-lb (250-kg) bombs.

Status: The MiG-21bis appeared in service with the Soviet Air Forces in 1975 as an upgraded derivative of the MiG-21MF (see 1974 edition).

Notes: The MiG-21bis (Fishbed-N) closely resembles the MiG-21MF (Fishbed-J) externally, but features updated avionics and systems, and introduces an R-25 engine in place of the lower-powered R-13 that powers earlier production versions of the fighter. The MiG-21bis is to be licence-manufactured in India with the production phase-out of the current MiG-21M from 1979. Although still essentially an air combat fighter, the MiG-21bis offers improved ground attack capability.

MIKOYAN MIG-21BIS (FISHED-N)

Dimensions: Span, 23 ft $5\frac{1}{2}$ in (7,15 m); length (including probe), 51 ft $8\frac{1}{2}$ in (15,76 m), (without probe), 44 ft 2 in (13,46 m); wing area, 247·57 sq ft (23,00 m²).

MIKOYAN MIG-23S (FLOGGER-B)

Country of Origin: USSR.

Type: Single-seat interceptor and air superiority fighter (and two-seat conversion trainer—Flogger-C).

Power Plant: One (estimated) 14,330 lb (6 500 kg) dry and 23,150 lb (10 500 kg) reheat Tumansky turbofan.

Performance: (Estimated) Max. speed, 865 mph (1 392 km/h) at 1,000 ft (305 m) or Mach 1·2, 1,520 mph (2 446 km/h) above 39,370 ft (12 000 m) or Mach 2·3; combat radius (intercept mission), 450 mls (725 km); normal max. range, 1,400 mls (2 250 km); ferry range (three 330 Imp gal/1 500 l external tanks), 2,485 mls (4 000 km) at 495 mph (796 km/h) or Mach 0·75.

Weights: (Estimated) Empty equipped, 18,000 lb (8 165 kg); normal loaded, 34,600 lb (15 700 kg); max. take-off, 39,130 lb (17 750 kg).

Armament: One 23-mm twin-barrel GSh-23 cannon plus two AA-7 Apex and two AA-8 Aphid AAMs.

Status: The MiG-23S reportedly entered service in the intercept and air superiority roles with the Soviet Air Forces in 1971, and upwards of 1,000 fighters of this type were believed to be in service by the beginning of 1978.

Notes: Several variants of the MiG-23 are currently in service, the principle of these being the MiG-23S (Flogger-B) described above and illustrated on opposite page, a tandem two-seat operational trainer, the MiG-23U (Flogger-C), and an export version of the single-seater (Flogger-E), which, illustrated above, has a smaller radar in a shorter nose and simplified avionics. The last-mentioned version has been widely exported, recipient countries including Egypt, Iraq, Libya and Syria. (See MiG-27 on pages 156–157.)

MIKOYAN MIG-23S (FLOGGER-B)

Dimensions: (Estimated) Span (max.), 46 ft 9 in (14,25 m), (min.), 27 ft 6 in (8,38 m); length (including probe), 55 ft 1½ in (16,80 m); wing area, 293·4 sq ft (27,26 m²).

MIKOYAN MIG-25 (FOXBAT)

Country of Origin: USSR.

Type: Single-seat interceptor fighter (Foxbat-A) and high-altitude reconnaissance aircraft (Foxbat-B).

Power Plant: Two (estimated) 17,640 lb (8 000 kg) dry and 24,250 lb (11 000 kg) reheat Tumansky turbojets.

Performance: (Estimated—Foxbat-A) Max. short-period dash speed, 1,850 mph (2 980 km/h) or Mach 2·8 above 36,000 ft (10 970 m); max. sea level speed, 650 mph (1 045 km/h) or Mach 0·85; mission radius (max. internal fuel), 590 mls (950 km); max. range, 1,240 mls (2 000 km); service ceiling, 72,180 ft (22 000 m).

Weights: Empty, 44,100 lb (20 000 kg); max. take-off, 77,160 lb (35 000 kg).

Armament: Four AA-6 Acrid AAMs (two infra-red homing and two semi-active radar homing).

Status: The MiG-25 commenced its development trials in the mid 'sixties and apparently entered service in the high-altitude intercept role in 1970—71, and in the reconnaissance role in 1972.

Notes: Three operational versions of the MiG-25 are known to exist, comprising a missile-armed high-altitude interceptor (Foxbat-A), a camera- and IR linescan-equipped reconnaissance model (Foxbat-B) and a SLAR (side-looking aircraft radar) equipped reconnaissance model (Foxbat-D). A two-seat conversion training version (Foxbat-C) possesses no operational capability. The Foxbat-B is illustrated above and the Foxbat-A is illustrated opposite.

MIKOYAN MIG-25 (FOXBAT)

Dimensions: Span, 45 ft 11 in (14,00 m); length (including probe), 73 ft 2 in (22,30 m); height, 18 ft $4\frac{1}{2}$ in (5,60 m); wing area, 602·78 sq ft (56,00 m²).

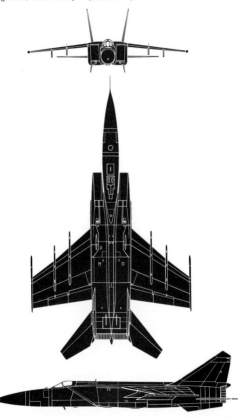

MIKOYAN MIG-27 (FLOGGER-D)

Country of Origin: USSR.

Type: Single-seat tactical strike fighter.

Power Plant: One (estimated) 15,500 lb (7 025 kg) dry and 20,500 lb (9 300 kg) reheat Tumansky turbofan.

Performance: (Estimated) Max. speed, 865 mph (1 392 km/h) at 1,000 ft (305 m) or Mach 1·2, 990 mph (1 590 km/h) above 39,370 ft (12 000 m) or Mach 1·5; combat radius (hi-lo-hi with centreline drop tank), 620 mls (1 000 km), (lo-lo-lo), 220 mls (350 km); normal max. range, 1,550 mls (2 500 km); ferry range (three 330 Imp gal/1 500 l drop tanks), 2,610 mls (4 200 km).

Weights: (Estimated) Empty equipped, 18,000 lb (8 165 kg); normal loaded, 35,275 lb (16 000 kg).

Armament: One 23-mm six-barrel rotary cannon and up to four AS-7 Kerry ASMs or various bombs up to 6,600 lb (total) on five external stations.

Status: A derivative of the MiG-23 interceptor, the MiG-27 is believed to have entered service in 1974.

Notes: The MiG-27 differs from the MiG-23S (see pages 152–153) in having simple fixed engine air intakes in place of variable-area intakes, a simpler, shorter exhaust nozzle for lower-boost reheat, a redesigned nose with laser rangefinder, a sturdier undercarriage with low-pressure tyres and bulged housings, and repositioned weapon pylons. The MiG-27 is optimised for the battlefield interdiction and counterair roles. An export model is referred to as the Flogger-F.

MIKOYAN MIG-27 (FLOGGER-D)

Dimensions: (Estimated) Span (max.), 46 ft 9 in (14,25 m), (min.), 27 ft 6 in (8,38 m); length (including probe), 54 ft 0 in (16,46 m); wing area, 293·4 sq ft (27,26 m²).

MITSUBISHI F-1

Country of Origin: Japan.

Type: Single-seat close air support fighter.

Power Plant: Two 4,710 lb (2.136 kg) dry and 7,070 lb (3.207 kg) reheat Ishikawajima-Harima TF40-IHI-801A (Rolls-Royce/Turboméca Adour) turbofans.

Performance: Max. speed, 1,056 mph (1.700 km/h) at 40,000 ft (12.190 m), or Mach 1·6; combat radius (internal fuel only plus four Sidewinder AAMs), 173 mls (278 km), lo-lo-lo (with eight 500-lb/226,8-kg bombs and two 180 Imp gal/820 l drop tanks), 218 mls (351 km), hi-lo-hi (with ASM-1 anti-shipping missiles and one 180 Imp gal/820 l drop tank), 346 mls (556 km); max. ferry range, 1,785 mls (2.870 km); max. climb, 35,000 ft/min (177,8 m/sec).

Weights: Operational empty, 14,017 lb (6.358 kg); max. take-off, 30,146 lb (13.674 kg).

Armament: One 20-mm Vulcan JM-61 multi-barrel cannon. Five external stores stations for up to 8,000 lb (3.629 kg) of ordnance. Detachable multiple ejector racks may be fitted for up to 12 500-lb (226,8-kg) bombs. Wingtip attachment points for two or four Sidewinder or Mitsubishi AAM-1 air-to-air missiles. Two Mitsubishi ASM-1 anti-shipping missiles may be carried.

Status: Two prototypes flown on June 3 and 7, 1975, respectively and first production aircraft flown on June 16, 1977. Forty-four ordered for Air Self-Defence Force by beginning of 1978 and additional 19 to be procured from Fiscal 1978 funds. Total procurement of 80 envisaged.

158

MITSUBISHI F-1

Dimensions: Span, 25 ft 10¼ in (7,88 m); length, 58 ft 7 in (17,86 m); height, 14 ft 4¾ in (4,39 m); wing area, 228 sq ft (21,18 m²).

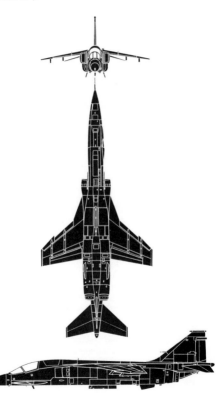

NDN AIRCRAFT NDN-1 FIRECRACKER

Country of Origin: United Kingdom.

Type: Tandem two-seat primary-basic trainer.

Power Plant: One 260 hp Avco Lycoming AEIO-540-B4D5 four-cylinder horizontally-opposed engine.

Performance: Max. speed, 211 mph (339 km/h); cruise (75% power), 201 mph (323 km/h) at 7,500 ft (2 285 m); range (no reserve), 1,584 mls (2 549 km); initial climb, 1,800 ft/min (9,1 m/sec); absolute ceiling, 20,000 ft (6 100 m).

Weights: Empty equipped, 1,830 lb (831 kg); max. take-off (aerobatic at 6g), 2,840 lb (1 288 kg).

Status: Prototype flown May 26, 1977. Intended as a "technology transfer" programme through which developing countries may establish their own aircraft industries, initially assembling the Firecracker and progressively taking over the manufacture of all detail parts and sub-assemblies, achieving completely indigenous production with the 61st aeroplane.

Notes: The Firecracker has been designed for series production without costly plant and equipment. Its construction calls for no forgings or extrusions and no parts (other than the glass-fibre cowlings and fairings) embody two-dimensional curvature. The entire airframe is built from light alloy or sheet steel and bar stock of readily available specifications, and all parts may be cold-formed by hand during construction. The Firecracker is fully aerobatic and provision is made for four pylons for external stores, suiting the aircraft for weapon training or light strike tasks. A hydraulically-operated air brake is provided beneath the fuselage and both crew seats are partly reclined to increase g tolerance.

NDN AIRCRAFT NDN-1 FIRECRACKER

Dimensions: Span, 26 ft 0 in (7,92 m); length, 25 ft 3 in (7,69 m); height, 9 ft 10 in (2,99 m); wing area, 126 sq ft (11,70 m²).

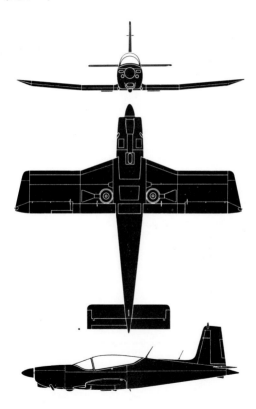

NORTHROP F-5E TIGER II

Country of Origin: USA.

Type: Single-seat air-superiority fighter.

Power Plant: Two 3,500 lb (1 588 kg) dry and 5,000 lb (2 268 kg) reheat General Electric J85-GE-21 turbojets.

Performance: Max. speed (at 13,220 lb/5 997 kg), 1,056 mph (1 700 km/h) or Mach 1·6 at 36,090 ft (11 000 m), 760 mph (1 223 km/h) or Mach 1·0 at sea level, (with wingtip missiles), 990 mph (1 594 km/h) or Mach 1·5 at 36,090 ft (11 000 m); combat radius (internal fuel), 173 mls (278 km), (with 229 Imp gal/1 041 l drop tank), 426 mls (686 km); initial climb (at 13,220 lb/5 997 kg), 31,600 ft/min (160,53 m/sec); combat ceiling, 53,500 ft (16 305 m).

Weights: Take-off (wingtip launching rail configuration), 15,400 lb (6 985 kg); max. take-off, 24,083 lb (10 924 kg).

Armament: Two 20-mm M-39 cannon with 280 rpg and two wingtip-mounted AIM-9 Sidewinder AAMs. Up to 7,000 lb (3 175 kg) of ordnance (for attack role).

Status: First F-5E flown August 11, 1972, and first deliveries February 1973. Some 780 (including F-5F) delivered by the beginning of 1978, when production (F-5E and F-5F) was running at 15 per month.

Notes: A more powerful derivative of the F-5A (see 1970 edition) optimised for the air-superiority role, the F-5E won the USAF's International Fighter Aircraft (IFA) contest in November 1970, and is being supplied under the Military Assistance Programme to South Korea, Taiwan, Thailand and Jordan. Orders for the F-5E have also been placed by eight other air forces, small numbers having also been supplied to the USAF and US Navy. The first two-seat F-5F flew on September 25, 1974, and production deliveries of this version began mid-1976. The F-5E may be fitted with a camera nose.

NORTHROP F-5E TIGER II

Dimensions: Span, 26 ft 8½ in (8,14 m); length, 48 ft 2½ in (14,69 m); height, 13 ft 4 in (4,06 m); wing area, 186·2 sq ft (17,29 m²).

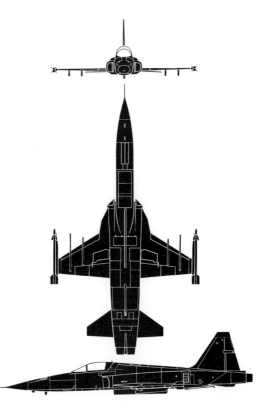

PANAVIA TORNADO

Countries of Origin: UK, Federal Germany and Italy.
Type: Two-seat multi-role fighter.
Power Plant: Two 8,500 lb (3 855 kg) dry and 15,000 lb (6 800 kg) reheat Turbo-Union RB.199-34R-4 Mk 101 turbofans.
Performance: (Estimated) Max. speed (clean), 840 mph (1 350 km/h) at 500 ft (150 m) or Mach 1·1, 1,385 mph (2 230 km/h) at 36,090 ft (11 000 m) or Mach 2·1; tactical radius (lo-lo-lo) with external stores, 450 mls (725 km), (hi-lo-hi) with external stores, 750 mls (1 200 km); max. ferry range, 3,000+ mls (4 830+ km).
Weights: (Estimated) Empty, 28,000 lb (12 700 kg); loaded (clean), 40,000 lb (18 145 kg); max. take-off, 55,000 lb (25 000 kg).
Armament: Two 27-mm Mauser cannon with 125 rpg and various ordnance combinations on seven (three fixed and four swivelling) external stores stations.
Status: First prototype flown on August 14, 1974, and a further eight prototypes plus first two of six pre-production aircraft flown by beginning of 1978, at which time production orders totalled 150 aircraft (78 for RAF, 57 for Luftwaffe and Marineflieger, and 15 for Italian Air Force) against planned tri-national procurement of 809 aircraft.
Notes: ADV (Air Defence Version) will comprise approx. 165 of RAF's total Tornado procurement of 385. To fly as a prototype early in 1979, it will have lengthened fuselage, a new Marconi-Elliot radar, uprated engines and four Skyflash AAMs.

164

PANAVIA TORNADO

Dimensions: Span (max.), 45 ft 8 in (13,90 m), (min.), 28 ft 3 in (8,60 m); length, 54 ft 9½ in (16,70 m); height, 18 ft 8½ in (5,70 m); wing area, 322·9 sq ft (30,00 m²).

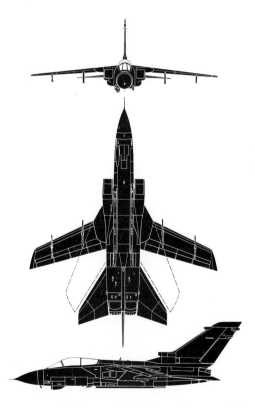

PARTENAVIA P.68R VICTOR

Country of Origin: Italy.
Type: Light utility and business executive transport.
Power Plant: Two 200 hp Avco Lycoming IO-360-A1B6 four-cylinder horizontally-opposed engines.
Performance: Max. speed, 212 mph (341 km/h) at sea level; cruise (75% power), 198 mph (319 km/h) at 7,500 ft (2 285 m), (65% power), 191 mph (307 km/h) at 11,000 ft (3 353 m), (55% power), 186 mph (299 km/h) at 12,000 ft (3 660 m); range (65% power and no reserves), 1,100 mls (1 770 km); initial climb, 1,660 ft/min (8,43 m/sec); service ceiling, 22,200 ft (6 765 m).
Weights: Max. take-off, 4,321 lb (1 960 kg).
Accommodation: Standard seating for six in three side-by-side pairs with dual controls for front pair. Optional bench seat for three in place of two rearmost seats.
Status: Prototype flown December 1976, with production commencing last quarter of 1977 and initial customer deliveries scheduled for mid-1978.
Notes: The P.68R differs from the P.68B Victor (see 1975 edition) primarily in having a retractable undercarriage, the main members retracting into bulged fairings, and a proposed development is the P.68RT with turbo-supercharged engines. More than 100 fixed-undercarriage Victors had been delivered by the beginning of 1978, the first prototype having flown on May 25, 1970, and the P.68B differed from the original production P.68 (see 1973 edition) in having a 6-in (15-cm) extension aft of the cockpit and improved instrumentation.

PARTENAVIA P.68R VICTOR

Dimensions: Span, 39 ft 4½ in (12,00 m); length, 30 ft 8 in (9,35 m); height, 11 ft 1¾ in (3,40 m); wing area, 200·2 sq ft (18,60 m²).

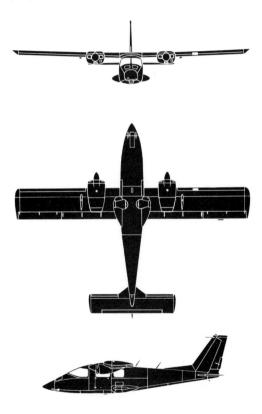

PIAGGIO P.166-DL3

Country of Origin: Italy.

Type: Light multi-purpose transport.

Power Plant: Two 587 shp Avco Lycoming LTP-101-600 turboprops.

Performance: (At 8,500 lb/3 855 kg) Max. speed, 259 mph (417 km/h) at 10,000 ft (3 050 m); max. cruise, 251 mph (404 km/h) at 10,000 ft (3 050 m); econ. cruise, 186 mph (300 km/h); range, 886–1,078 mls (1 426–1 736 km), (with optional underwing tanks and 30 min reserve), 1,364–1,657 mls (2 195–2 668 km); initial climb, 2,080 ft/min (10,6 m/sec); service ceiling, 26,000 ft (7 925 m).

Weights: Basic empty, 4,688 lb (2 126 kg); max. take-off, 9,480 lb (4 300 kg).

Accommodation: Normal flight crew of two and eight passengers in typical arrangement.

Status: Prototype flown July 3, 1976, with production of initial batch of four aircraft initiated 1977.

Notes: The P.166-DL3 is a turboprop-powered derivative of the piston-engined P.166-BL2 (380 hp Avco Lycoming IGSO-540s), and has been preceded by 110 examples of earlier P.166 variants, including the P.166M for the Italian Air Force and the P.166S search and surveillance version for the South African Air Force. By use of quick-change kits, the P.166-DL3 can be used as a business executive transport (with up to eight passengers in the main cabin), as a paratroop transport (up to 10 fully-equipped paratroops), as an aeromedical transport (with two casualty stretchers and two medical attendants) and as a multi-engined trainer. Four wing strong points permit the carriage of external stores for search and rescue, counter-insurgency, etc.

PIAGGIO P.166-DL3

Dimensions: Span, 48 ft 2 in (14,69 m); length, 39 ft 0 in (11,90 m); height, 16 ft 5 in (5,00 m); wing area, 285·9 sq ft (26,56 m²).

PILATUS PC-7 TURBO TRAINER

Country of Origin: Switzerland.

Type: Tandem two-seat basic-advanced trainer.

Power Plant: One 680 shp (derated to 515 shp) Pratt & Whitney (Canada) PT6A-25A turboprop.

Performance: Max. speed, 248 mph (400 km/h) at sea level, 270 mph (435 km/h) at 16,405 ft (5 000 m); range cruise (60% power), 186 mph (300 km/h) at sea level, 193 mph (310 km/h) at 16,405 ft (5 000 m); max. range (60% power with 20 min plus 5% reserves), 683 mls (1 100 km); initial climb (at 4,189 lb/1 900 kg), 2,066 ft/min.

Weights: Empty, 2,822 lb (1 280 kg); loaded (aerobatic), 4,189 lb (1 900 kg); max. take-off, 5.952 lb (2 700 kg).

Armament: Aircraft supplied by parent company with no provision for armament, but six hardpoints incorporated in wing permitting external loads of up to 2,292 lb (1 040 kg).

Status: First PC-7 prototype flown on April 12, 1966, with second flying May 1975. Initial series of 35 initiated 1977 with first production aircraft built against orders from Burma and Bolivia scheduled for completion in May 1978. Production rate of four–five monthly planned for 1979. Marketing collaboration being provided by Dornier GmbH of Germany.

Notes: The PC-7 has been derived from the piston-engined PC-3 and, apart from having a turboprop, introduces an extensively revised structure and fuel system, modernised cockpits and various aerodynamic refinements. The PC-7 is envisaged as a successor to the P-3 in Swiss service from the mid-'eighties.

PILATUS PC-7 TURBO TRAINER

Dimensions: Span, 34 ft 1½ in (10,40 m); length, 31 ft 11$\frac{9}{10}$ in (9,75 m); height, 10 ft 6⅓ in (3,21 m); wing area, 176·68 sq ft (16,60 m²).

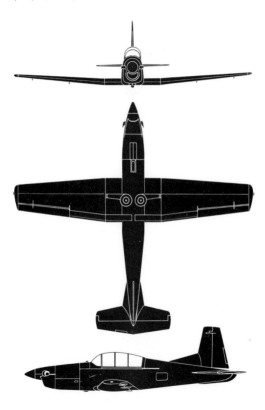

PIPER PA 32RT-300T TURBO LANCE II

Country of Origin: USA.

Type: Light cabin monoplane.

Power Plant: One 300 hp Avco Lycoming TIO-540-S1AD turbo-supercharged six-cylinder horizontally-opposed engine.

Performance: Max. speed, 222 mph (358 km/h) at optimum altitude; cruise (75% power), 201 mph (324 km/h), (55% power), 159 mph (256 km/h); range (with 45 min reserve), 852 mls (1 371 km) at 75% power, 875 mls (1 414 km) at 65% power, 938 mls (1 510 km) at 55% power; initial climb, 1,000 ft (5,08 m/sec).

Weights: Empty equipped, 1,529 lb (693 kg); loaded, 3,600 lb (1 633 kg).

Accommodation: Six persons in pairs in individual seats with dual controls as standard. Two baggage compartments with total capacity of 200 lb (90,7 kg).

Status: Introduced in October 1977 as a turbo-supercharged variant of the Lance II launched simultaneously, these being the 1978 models of what was previously known as the Chero-kee Lance, this having been flown as a prototype on August 30, 1974.

Notes: The Lance combines the fuselage and heavy-duty undercarriage of the PA 34 Seneca II with components of the fixed-undercarriage PA 32-300 Cherokee Six 300, and the Lance II and Turbo Lance differ from earlier models primarily in having a small T-type tail assembly.

PIPER PA 32RT-300T TURBO LANCE II

Dimensions: Span, 32 ft 9½ in (10,00 m); length, 28 ft 10⅘ in (8,81 m); height, 9 ft 6 in (2,90 m); wing area, 174·5 sq ft (16,21 m²).

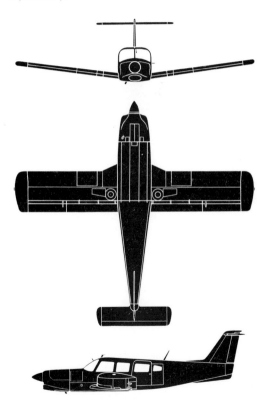

PIPER PA 38 TOMAHAWK

Country of Origin: USA.
Type: Side-by-side two-seat primary trainer.
Power Plant: One 112 bhp Avco Lycoming 0-235-L2C four-cylinder horizontally-opposed engine.
Performance: Max. speed, 130 mph (209 km/h) at sea level; cruise (75% power), 125 mph (202 km/h) at 8,800 ft (2 680 m), (65% power), 117 mph (189 km/h) at 11,500 ft (3 505 m); range (with 45 min reserve), 463 mls (745 km) at 75% power, 500 mls (807 km) at 65% power; initial climb, 700 ft/min (3,55 m/sec); service ceiling, 12,850 ft (3 917 m).
Weights: Empty equipped, 1,064 lb (483 kg); max. take-off, 1,670 lb (757 kg).
Status: The PA 38 Tomahawk trainer was announced in October 1977 for customer deliveries commencing January 1978.
Notes: Placing emphasis on simplicity of maintenance and low operating costs, the Tomahawk incorporates a high degree of component interchangeability and several design features considered innovative in aircraft of its category. Like the Beechcraft Model 77 (see 1977 edition), with which the new Piper trainer is directly competitive, the Tomahawk employs a T-tail, which is claimed to afford greater stability and more positive rudder control, and its high aspect ratio wing of constant chord and thickness utilises an adaptation of the NASA Whitcomb aerofoil which offers high lift characteristics.

PIPER PA 38 TOMAHAWK

Dimensions: Span, 34 ft 0 in (10,36 m); length, 23 ft 1¼ in (7,04 m); height, 8 ft 7½ in (2,63 m); wing area, 125 sq ft (11,61 m²).

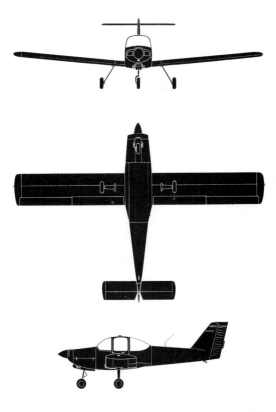

PIPER PA 42 CHEYENNE III

Country of Origin: USA.

Type: Light business executive transport.

Power Plant: Two 680 shp (de-rated from 850 shp) Pratt & Whitney (Canada) PT6A-41 turboprops.

Performance: Max. cruise, 330 mph (532 km/h) at 15,000 ft (4 570 m), 347 mph (558 km/h) at 20,000 ft (6 095 m); max. range, 1,658 mls (2 668 km) at 15,000 ft (4 570 m), 1,968 mls (3 167 km) at 25,000 ft (7 620 m); initial climb, 2,450 ft/min (12,44 m/sec); service ceiling, 30,500 ft (9 295 m).

Weights: Empty equipped, 5,621 lb (2 550 kg); max. take-off, 10,550 lb (4 785 kg).

Accommodation: Flight crew of one or two on separate flight deck with four—eight passengers in cabin.

Status: The PA 42 Cheyenne III was introduced in September 1977, with customer deliveries scheduled for mid-1978.

Notes: The original PA-31T Cheyenne prototype flew on August 20, 1969, with customer deliveries commencing in 1974, the original model currently being offered as the Cheyenne I with 500 shp PT6A-11s and as the Cheyenne II with 620 shp PT6A-28s. The PA 42 Cheyenne III is an extensively redesigned model with more powerful engines, enlarged overall dimensions and a tail of the increasingly fashionable T-type.

176

PIPER PA 42 CHEYENNE III

Dimensions: Span, 47 ft 8⅛ in (914,53 m); length, 38 ft 0 in (11,58 m); height, 11 ft 9½ in (3,61 m); wing area, 293 sq ft (27,200 m²).

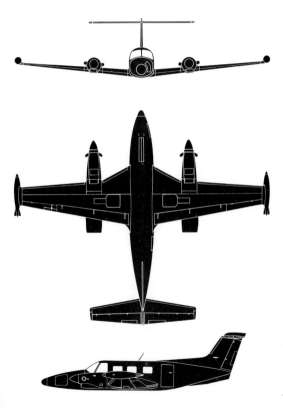

PROCAER F 15F DELFINO

Country of Origin: Italy.

Type: Side-by-side two-seat primary-basic trainer.

Power Plant: One 200 hp Avco Lycoming IO-360-A1B1 four-cylinder horizontally-opposed engine.

Performance: Max. speed, 193 mph (310 km/h); cruise, 174 mph (280 km/h); endurance (typical training mission), 4·5 hrs; initial climb, 984 ft/min (5,0 m/sec); service ceiling, 17,060 ft (5 200 m).

Weights: Empty equipped, 1,653 lb (750 kg); max. take-off (aerobatic), 2,160 lb (980 kg), (normal category), 2,643 lb (1 200 kg).

Status: Prototype flown in July 1977. Provisional planning for initiation of small production batch mid-1978.

Notes: The F-15F Delfino primary-cum-basic trainer is a derivative of the well-known all-metal four-seat F 15E Picchio cabin monoplane certificated in 1970. Designed by Stelio Frati, the F 15 Picchio flew in prototype form for the first time on May 7, 1959, and was followed by small production batches of the 180 hp F 15A, the F 15B with increased wing area, the 260 hp F 15C and the 285 hp F 15E which was the first model of all-metal construction. Production of the F 15 Picchio exceeded 70 aircraft by the beginning of 1978. The F 15F retains the all-metal structure of the F 15E but has a new one-piece aft-sliding canopy and is offered with optional fixed undercarriage and wingtip tanks. It is intended primarily to meet the need of a low-cost primary-cum-basic military trainer.

PROCAER F 15F DELFINO

Dimensions: Span, 32 ft 6 in (9,90 m); length, 24 ft 10 in (7,58 m); height, 9 ft 2½ in (2,80 m); wing area, 143 sq ft (13,30 m²).

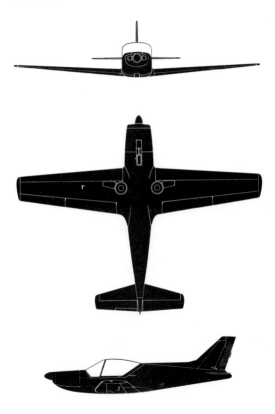

PZL M-18 DROMADER

Country of Origin: Poland.
Type: Single-seat agricultural aircraft.
Power Plant: One 1,000 hp WSK-PZL-Kalisz (Shvetsov) ASh-62IR nine-cylinder radial air-cooled engine.
Performance: (At 9,259 lb/4 200 kg) Max. speed (clean configuration), 159 mph (256 km/h), (with spreader bar), 147 mph (237 km/h); max. cruise, 127 mph (205 km/h), (with spreader bar), 118 mph (190 km/h); operating speed, 105–115 mph (170–185 km/h); range (no reserve), 323 mls (520 km); initial climb, 1,142 ft/min (5,8 m/sec), (with spreader bar), 1,043 ft/min (5,3 m/sec); service ceiling, 21,325 ft (6 500 m).
Weights: Empty, 5,445 lb (2 470 kg); normal loaded, 9,529 lb (4 200 kg); max. take-off, 11,684 lb (5 300 kg).
Status: First of three prototypes flown late 1976. Production deliveries planned for late 1978.
Notes: The Dromader (Dromedary) has been developed with the co-operation of Rockwell International and does, in fact, utilise Rockwell International Thrush Commander outer wing panels. The Dromader has a 550 Imp gal (2 500 l) epoxy fibre-glass hopper forward of the cockpit. A Transland spreader for dusting with dry chemical or eight atomisers for fine spraying may be fitted, and the aircraft can also utilise the Rockwell International water bombing installation for fire suppression. The Dromader is of all-metal construction and emphasis in the design has been placed on pilot safety, the cockpit being able to withstand forward forces of up to 40 g and all fuel is located in the outer wing panels. All elements of the structure exposed to contact with agricultural chemicals are treated with polyurethane or epoxy enamels, or are of stainless steel.

PZL M-18 DROMADER

Dimensions: Span, 58 ft 0⅘ in (17,70 m); length, 31 ft 2 in (9,50 m); height, 10 ft 2 in (3,10 m); wing area, 430·56 sq ft (40,00 m²).

RFB FANTRAINER AWI-2

Country of Origin: Federal Germany.
Type: Tandem two-seat basic trainer.
Power Plant: Two 150 hp Audi-NSU Wankel EA 871-L rotating piston engines driving a ducted fan.
Performance: (Estimated) Max. speed, 220 mph (354 km/h) at sea level, 196 mph (315 km/h) at 20,000 ft (6 095 m); max. range (no reserves), 1,610 mls (2 590 km) at 20,000 ft (6 095 m); initial climb, 1,450 ft/min (7,36 m/sec).
Weights: Operational empty, 2,017 lb (915 kg); max. take-off, 2,976 lb (1 350 kg).
Status: First of two prototypes commenced its flight test programme October 1977.
Notes: The Fantrainer, by use of an integrated ducted-fan propulsion system, will simulate the characteristics of turbojet-powered aircraft but offers appreciably lower operating costs and is intended to cover all phases of the training spectrum up to such types as the Alpha Jet. Two prototypes of the AWI-2 version of the Fantrainer have been ordered by the Federal Germany Ministry of Defence and these have essentially similar cockpits to those of the Alpha Jet (see pages 62–63). The coupled Wankel engines may be replaced by a single turboshaft of 400 eshp upwards, this variant of the Fantrainer being the ATI-2, and alternative wings are offered: application of a 34 ft 5$\frac{1}{3}$ in (10,50 m) wing resulting in the AWI-4 and ATI-4, and use of a 25 ft 10$\frac{1}{4}$ in (7,88 m) wing producing the ATI-2K1.

RFB FANTRAINER AWI-2

Dimensions: Span, 31 ft 5$\frac{9}{10}$ in (9,60 m); length, 26 ft 3$\frac{3}{4}$ in (8,02 m); height, 9 ft 6$\frac{1}{8}$ in (2,90 m); wing area, 149·6 sq ft (13,90 m²).

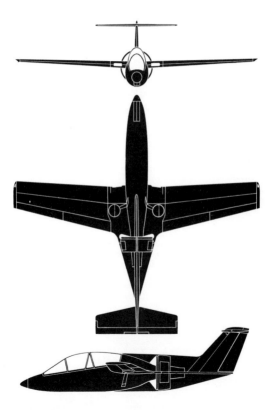

ROCKWELL INTERNATIONAL
(FUJI) COMMANDER 700

Countries of Origin: USA and Japan.

Type: Light cabin monoplane.

Power Plant: Two 340 hp Avco Lycoming TIO-540-R2AD six-cylinder horizontally-opposed engines.

Performance: Max. speed, 266 mph (428 km/h) at 20,000 ft (6 095 m); cruise (75% power), 252 mph (405 km/h) at 24,000 ft (7 315 m), (at 45% power), 177 mph (285 km/h) at 15,000 ft (4 570 m); initial climb, 1,460 ft/min (7,4 m/sec); range (at 75% power), 810 mls (1 303 km).

Weights: Empty equipped, 4,400 lb (1 995 kg); max. take-off, 6,600 lb (2 993 kg).

Accommodation: Pilot and co-pilot in individual seats and four to six passengers in separate pressurised cabin.

Status: The result of a joint programme by Rockwell International (USA) and Fuji (Japan), the first of four prototypes having flown (in Japan) on November 13, 1975, and the second (in the USA) on February 25, 1976. Subsequent test programme shared with three pre-production aircraft (one in Japan and two in USA) and customer deliveries were expected to commence early 1978.

Notes: The Commander 700 (known in Japan as the FA-300) is a joint programme under which the respective participants will be responsible for the assembly of all aircraft for sale in their defined marketing areas. A version with 450 hp engines, the Commander 710 (FA-300-KAI) built by Fuji, was flown in Japan on 22 December 1976.

ROCKWELL INTERNATIONAL (FUJI) COMMANDER 700

Dimensions: Span, 42 ft 5½ in (12,94 m); length, 39 ft 4½ in (12,00 m); height, 12 ft 9½ in (3,90 m); wing area, 200·2 sq ft (18,60 m²).

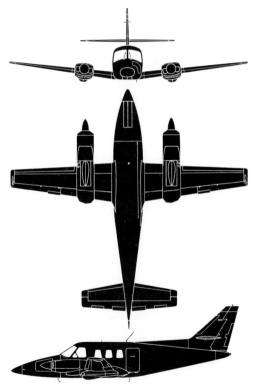

ROCKWELL INTERNATIONAL XFV-12A

Country of Origin: USA.

Type: Technology development aircraft.

Power Plant: One 16,400 lb (7 438 kg) dry 28,090 lb (12 742 kg) reheat Pratt & Whitney F401-PW-400 turbofan.

Performance: (Estimated) Max. speed, 990–1,055 mph (1 590–1 700 km/h) above 36,000 ft (10 970 m), or Mach 1·5–1·6; range (after 300-ft/91-m take-off roll), 1,000+ mls (1 610+ km).

Weights: Empty equipped, 13,800 lb (6 260 kg); max. vertical take-off, 19,500 lb (8 845 kg); max. short take-off, 24,250 lb (11 000 kg).

Status: Sole prototype rolled out August 26, 1977, and initial tethered hover tests initiated prior to year's end. Conventional flight testing scheduled to commence during second quarter of 1978.

Notes: The XFV-12A is an advanced technology development aircraft utilising the thrust-augmented wing (TAW) concept, an integrated lift/propulsion/control system. Engine exhaust air is ducted to augmenter flaps in the foreplane and wings and directed downwards through slot nozzles, primary and ambient air being mixed to increase vertical thrust over that obtainable from the engine airflow alone by more than 50%. Hovering control is achieved by varying the differential lift generated by the augmenter flaps and foreplane. Approximately 35% of the structure of the XFV-12A has been derived from existing aircraft (e.g., the A-4 Skyhawk and F-4 Phantom) and this research aircraft is intended to eventually lead to an operational ship-board fighter for use from small ships.

ROCKWELL INTERNATIONAL XFV-12A

Dimensions: Span, 28 ft 6 in (8,68 m); length, 43 ft 9½ in (13,36 m); height, 10 ft 4 in (3,15 m); wing area, 293 sq ft (27,20 m²).

ROCKWELL INTERNATIONAL
SABRELINER 65

Country of Origin: USA.

Type: Light business executive transport.

Power Plant: Two 3,700 lb (1 678 kg) Garrett AiResearch TFE 731-3-1D turbofans.

Performance: Max. speed, 528 mph (850 km/h), or Mach 0·8; recommended cruise, 495 mph (796 km/h), or Mach 0·75; long-range cruise, 462 mph (743 km/h), or Mach 0·7; range (four passengers and VFR reserve), 3,328 mls (5 354 km); initial climb, 3,540 ft/min (20 m/sec); cruise altitude, 39,000 ft (11 890 m).

Weights: Empty equipped, 13,330 lb (6 046 kg); max. take-off, 23,800 lb (10 795 kg).

Accommodation: Normal flight crew of two and basic cabin arrangements for seven, eight or ten passengers.

Status: First pre-production prototype Sabreliner 65 flown June 29, 1977, with second scheduled to fly June 1978. Customer deliveries expected to commence April 1979, with production rate of two per month for remainder of year.

Notes: The Sabreliner 65 is a progressive development of the Sabreliner 60 (see 1968 edition) with turbofans and utilising supercritical aerofoil technology, plain flaps being replaced by Fowler-type flaps, spoilers replacing the centreline air brake, an aft fuselage fuel tank being introduced and wing fuel capacity being increased. Similar changes are to be incorporated in the larger Sabreliner 75A (see 1975 edition) and deliveries of this model, to be known as the Sabreliner 80A, are scheduled to commence in December 1979.

ROCKWELL INTERNATIONAL SABRELINER 65

Dimensions: Span, 50 ft 1 in (15,26 m); length, 46 ft 11 in (14,30 m); height, 16 ft 0 in (4,88 m).

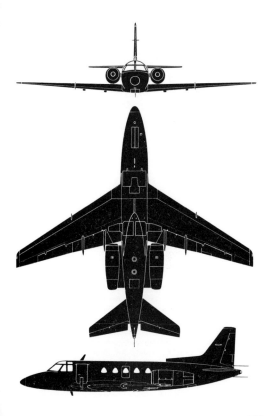

SAAB (JA) 37 VIGGEN

Country of Origin: Sweden.

Type: Single-seat all-weather intercepter fighter with secondary strike capability.

Power Plant: One 16,203 lb (7 350 kg) dry and 28,108 lb (12 750 kg) reheat Volvo Flygmotor RM 8B.

Performance: (Estimated) Max. speed (with two RB 24 Sidewinder AAMs), 1,320 mph (2 125 km/h) above 36,090 ft (11 000 m) or Mach 2·0, 910 mph (1 465 km/h) at 1,000 ft (305 m) or Mach 1·2; operational radius (M = 2·0 intercept with two AAMs), 250 mls (400 km), (lo-lo-lo ground attack with six Mk. 82 bombs), 300 mls (480 km); time (from brakes off) to 32,810 ft (10 000 m), 1·4 min.

Weights: (Estimated) Empty, 26,895 lb (12 200 kg); loaded (two AAMs), 37,040 lb (16 800 kg); max. take-off, 49,600 lb (22 500 kg).

Armament: One semi-externally mounted 30-mm Oerlikon KCA cannon with 150 rounds and up to 13,227 lb (6 000 kg) of ordnance on seven external stores stations.

Status: First of four JA 37 prototypes (modified from AJ 37 airframes) flown June 1974, with fifth prototype built from outset to JA 37 standards flown December 15, 1975. Initial production JA 37 flown on November 4, 1977.

Notes: The JA 37 is a development of the AJ 37 (see 1973 edition) which is optimised for the attack role, the SF 37 (see 1974 edition) and SH 37 being respectively tactical reconnaissance and sea surveillance derivatives of the latter. The JA 37 has uprated turbofan, cannon armament and X-Band Pulse Doppler radar.

SAAB (JA) 37 VIGGEN

Dimensions: Span, 34 ft $9\frac{1}{4}$ in (10,60 m); length (excluding probe), 50 ft $8\frac{1}{4}$ in (15,45 m); height, 19 ft $4\frac{1}{4}$ in (5,90 m); wing area (including foreplanes), 561·88 sq ft (52,20 m²).

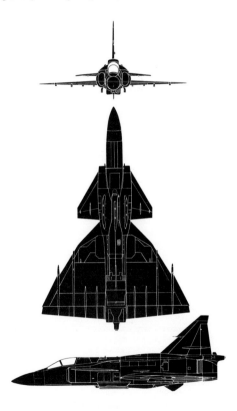

SEPECAT JAGUAR G.R. MK. 1

Countries of Origin: France and United Kingdom.
Type: Single-seat tactical strike fighter.
Power Plant: Two 4,620 lb (2 100 kg) dry and 7,140 lb (3 240 kg) reheat Rolls-Royce Turboméca RT.172 Adour 102 turbofans.
Performance: (At typical weight) Max. speed, 820 mph (1 320 km/h) or Mach 1·1 at 1,000 ft (305 m), 1,057 mph (1 700 km/h) or Mach 1·6 at 32,810 ft (10 000 m); cruise with max. ordnance, 430 mph (690 km/h) or Mach 0·65 at 39,370 ft (12 000 m); range with external fuel for lo-lo-lo mission profile, 450 mls (724 km), for hi-lo-hi mission profile, 710 mls (1 142 km); ferry range, 2,270 mls (3 650 km).
Weights: Normal take-off, 23,000 lb (10 430 kg); max. take-off, 32,600 lb (14 790 kg).
Armament: Two 30-mm Aden cannon and up to 10,000 lb (4 536 kg) ordnance on five external hardpoints.
Status: First of eight prototypes flown September 8, 1968. First production Jaguar E for France flown November 2, 1971, with first Jaguar A following April 20, 1972. First production Jaguar S for UK flown October 11, 1972. By the beginning of 1978, all 202 ordered by the UK had been delivered, together with some 150 of the 170 so far ordered by France, and deliveries of 12 Jaguar Internationals for each of Oman and Ecuador were continuing.
Notes: French versions are the single-seat A (*Appui Tactique*) and two-seat E (*École de Combat*), British versions being the single-seat S(G.R. Mk. 1) and two-seat B (T. Mk. 2). The export Jaguar International has uprated Adour 804 engines and these are also replacing Adour 102s in RAF Jaguars under a retrofit programme commencing during 1978. Matra Magic AAMs can be carried on overwing pylons.

SEPECAT JAGUAR G.R. MK. 1

Dimensions: Span, 28 ft 6 in (8,69 m); length, 50 ft 11 in (15,52 m); height, 16 ft 0½ in (4,89 m); wing area, 260·3 sq ft (24,18 m²).

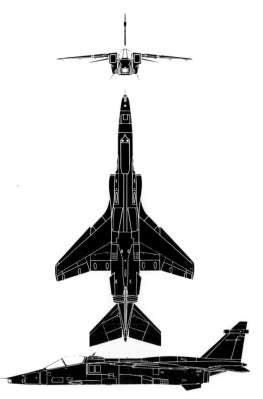

SHORTS 330

Country of Origin: United Kingdom.

Type: Third-level airliner and utility transport.

Power Plant: Two 1,173 shp Pratt & Whitney (Canada) PT6A-45A turboprops.

Performance: Max. cruise, 221 mph (356 km/h) at 10,000 ft (3 050 m); range cruise, 184 mph (296 km/h) at 10,000 ft; range (with 30 passengers and baggage, no reserve), 450 mls (725 km), (typical freighter configuration with 7,500-lb/ 3 400 kg payload), 368 mls (592 km); max range (passenger configuration with 4,060-lb/1 840-kg payload), 1,013 mls (1 630 km), (freighter configuration with 5,400-lb/2 450-kg payload), 1,013 mls (1 630 km); max. climb, 1,210 ft/min (6,14 m/sec).

Weights: Empty equipped (for 30 passengers), 14,500 lb (6 577 kg); max. take-off, 22,400 lb (10 160 kg).

Accommodation: Standard flight crew of two and normal accommodation for 30 passengers in 10 rows three abreast and 1,000 lb (455 kg) of baggage.

Status: Engineering prototype flown August 22, 1974, with production prototype following on July 8, 1975. First production aircraft flown on December 15, 1975. Customer deliveries commenced mid-1976, and at beginning of 1978, when long-lead items had been ordered for 35 aircraft, the Shorts 330 was serving with Time Air of Canada, Command Airways and Golden West Airlines of the USA, and DLT of Federal Germany with combined orders for 10 aircraft, and two (with two more on option) had been ordered by Henson Aviation of the USA.

Notes: A proposed maritime surveillance version is the SD3-MR Seeker with nose-mounted radar, search-and-rescue equipment, etc.

SHORTS 330

Dimensions: Span, 74 ft 8 in (22,76 m); length, 58 ft 0½ in (17,69 m); height, 16 ft 3 in (4,95 m); wing area, 453 sq ft (42,10 m²).

SUKHOI SU-15VD (FLAGON-F)

Country of Origin: USSR.

Type: Single-seat all-weather interceptor fighter.

Power Plant: Two 17,195 lb (7 800 kg) dry and 24,700 lb (11 200 kg) reheat Lyulka AL-21 turbojets.

Performance: (Estimated) Max. speed (clean configuration), 1,650 mph (2 755 km/h) above 36,000 ft (10 970 m), or Mach 2·5, (high drag configuration: e.g., drop tanks on fuselage stations and AA-6 Acrid AAMs on wing stations), 1,120 mph (1 800 km/h), or Mach 1·7; tactical radius (internal fuel), 450 mls (725 km); time to 36,000 ft (10 970 m), 2·5 min.

Weights: (Estimated) Empty equipped, 28,000 lb (12 700 kg); max. take-off, 45,000 lb (20 410 kg).

Armament: Two AA-3 Anab or AA-6 Acrid radar-guided air-to-air missiles on underwing pylons.

Status: The Su-15 apparently flew in prototype form during 1964-65, entering service with the IAP-VO Strany (the fighter element of the Anti-aircraft Defence of the Homeland) in 1969. It has since been progressively developed, the latest known service version being the Su-15VD (Flagon-F).

Notes: The initial production version of the Su-15, the Flagon-A, employed a plain delta wing similar to that of the earlier Su-11 (Fishpot-C), but this gave place on the next production model (Flagon-D) to a wing of extended span employing compound sweep, variants of this being an experimental STOL (short-take-off-and-landing) technology development version featuring three vertical lift jets mounted centrally in the fuselage (Flagon-B) and a tandem two-seat conversion training version (Flagon-C). Further wing modifications were introduced by the next single-seat production model (Flagon-E), illustrated above, and the latest version (Flagon-F), described above and illustrated opposite, has new radar in an ogival rather than conical nose and uprated engines.

SUKHOI SU-15VD (FLAGON-F)

Dimensions: (Estimated) Span, 34 ft 5 in (10,50 m); length, 70 ft 6 in (20,50 m); height, 16 ft 6 in (5,00 m); wing area, 387 sq ft (36,00 m²).

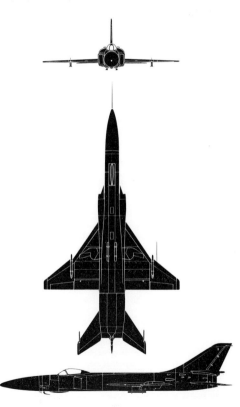

SUKHOI SU-17 (FITTER-C)

Country of Origin: USSR.

Type: Single-seat tactical strike fighter.

Power Plant: One 17,195 lb (7 800 kg) dry and 24,700 lb (11 200 kg) reheat Lyulka AL-21F-3 turbojet.

Performance: Max. speed (clean), 808 mph (1 300 km/h) or Mach 1·06 at sea level, 1,430 mph (2 300 km/h) at 39,370 ft (12 000 m) or Mach 2·17; combat radius (lo-lo-lo mission profile), 260 mls (420 km), (hi-lo-hi mission profile), 373 mls (600 km); range (with 2,205-lb/1 000-kg weapon load and auxiliary fuel), 1,415 mls (2 280 km); service ceiling, 57,415 ft (17 500 m).

Weights: Max. take-off, 39,022 lb (17 700 kg).

Armament: Two 30-mm NR-30 cannon with 70 rpg and (for short-range missions) a max. external ordnance load of 7,716 lb (3 500 kg). Typical external stores include UV-16-57 or UV-32-57 rocket pods containing 16 and 32 55-mm S-5 rockets respectively, 240-mm S-24 rockets, two AS-7 Kerry ASMs, or 550-lb (250-kg) or 1,100-lb (500-kg) bombs.

Status: The Su-17 entered service with the Soviet Air Forces in 1972, and is currently being exported to Warsaw Pact countries.

Notes: The Su-17 is a variable-geometry derivative of the Su-7 Fitter-A (see 1973 edition). Intended primarily for the close air support, battlefield interdiction and counterair roles, but with secondary combat zone air superiority capability, the Su-17 has been offered for export under the designations Su-20 and Su-22 (the latter being purchased by Peru), these differing in equipment standards, and the latest variant (Fitter-D) has a laser target seeker in a housing beneath the nose.

SUKHOI SU-17 (FITTER-C)

Estimated Dimensions: Span (max.), 45 ft 0 in (13,70 m), (min.), 32 ft 6 in (9,90 m); length (including probe), 57 ft 0 in (17,37 m); height, 15 ft 5 in (4,70 m).

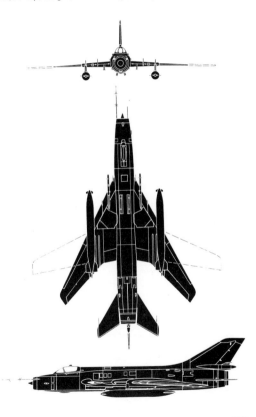

SUKHOI SU-19 (FENCER-A)

Country of Origin: USSR.

Type: Two-seat ground attack fighter.

Power Plant: Two (estimated) 13,230 lb (6 000 kg) dry and 19,840 lb (9 000 kg) reheat turbojets.

Performance: (Estimated) Max. speed, 760–840 mph (1 225–1 350 km/h) at sea level or Mach 1·0–1·1, 1,385–1,520 mph (2 230–2 445 km/h) at 36,090 ft (11 000 m) or Mach 2·1–2·3; radius of action (lo-lo-lo), 250 mls (400 km), (hi-lo-hi), 750 mls (1 200 km); max. endurance, 3–4 hrs.

Weights: (Estimated) Empty equipped, 33,000 lb (14 970 kg); max. take-off, 68,000 lb (30 845 kg).

Armament: One six-barrel 23-mm rotary cannon in the underside of the fuselage and up to 10,000–11,000 lb (4 500–5 000 kg) of ordnance on six external stations (two under the fuselage and four under the fixed wing glove), a typical ordnance load comprising two 1,100-lb (500-kg) bombs, two surface-to-air missiles and two pods each containing 16 or 32 57-mm unguided rockets.

Status: Prototypes of the Su-19 are believed to have flown in 1970, and this type was first reported to be in service with the Soviet Air Forces during the course of 1974. Western intelligence agencies indicated that some two hundred will have attained service by mid-1978.

Notes: The Su-19 (the accompanying illustrations of which should be considered as provisional) is the first Soviet fighter optimised for the ground attack role to have achieved service status. Wing leading-edge sweep varies from approximately 23 deg fully spread to 70 deg fully swept, and the wings reportedly incorporate both leading- and trailing-edge lift devices and lift dumpers acting as spoilers in conjunction with differential tail-plane movement for roll control.

SUKHOI SU-19 (FENCER-A)

Dimensions: (Estimated): Span (max.), 56 ft (17,00 m), (min.), 31 ft (9,45 m); length, 70 ft (21,35 m).

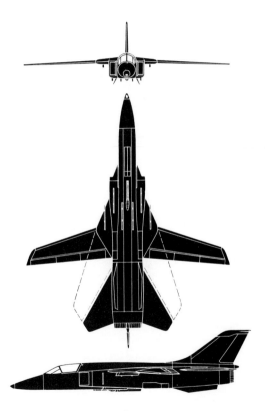

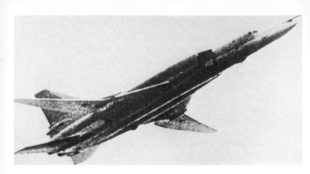

TUPOLEV (BACKFIRE-B)

Country of Origin: USSR.

Type: Strategic bomber.

Power Plant: Two (estimated) 33,070 lb (15 000 kg) dry and 46,300 lb (21 000 kg) reheat Kuznetsov turbofans.

Performance: (Estimated) Max. speed, 685 mph (1 100 km/h) or Mach 0·9 at sea level, 1,320 mph (2 125 km/h) at 39,370 ft (12 000 m) or Mach 2·0; combat radius (lo-lo-lo), 1,240 mls (2 000 km), (hi-lo-hi), 2,485 mls (4 000 km), (hi-hi-hi), 3,730 mls (6 000 km); service ceiling, 59,000 ft (18 000 m).

Weights: (Estimated) Empty equipped, 121,255 lb (55 000 kg); max. take-off, 297,625 lb (135 000 kg).

Armament: (Defensive) Remotely-controlled 23-mm cannon in tail barbette. Internal bomb load of up to 16,000 lb (7 250 kg) or two externally-mounted 9,920-lb (4 500-kg) AS-6 stand-off missiles with (approx.) 460-mile (740-km) range and inertial guidance.

Status: First reported in prototype form in 1969, the Backfire began to enter service with both the Soviet long-range aviation component and the Naval Air Force during the course of 1974, production reportedly running at 15 per year at the beginning of 1978 when 80–90 were believed in service.

Notes: The Backfire-B (the design bureau designation of which was unknown at the time of closing for press) has been the subject of considerable contention in relation to the Strategic Arms Limitation Talks (SALT), the Soviet Union alleging that it does not possess intercontinental range.

TUPOLEV (BACKFIRE-B)

Dimensions: (Estimated) Span (max.), 115 ft 0 in (35,00 m), (min.), 92 ft 0 in (28,00 m); length, 138 ft 0 in (42,00 m); height, 29 ft 6 in (9,00 m).

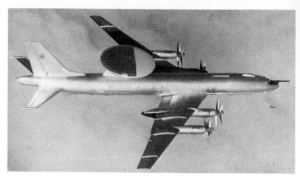

TUPOLEV TU-126 (MOSS)

Country of Origin: USSR.

Type: Airborne warning and control system aircraft.

Power Plant: Four 14,795 ehp Kuznetsov NK-12MV turbo-props.

Performance: (Estimated) Max. speed, 510 mph (820 km/h); max. continuous cruise, 460 mph (740 km/h) at 25,000 ft (7 620 m); operational cruise, 410 mph (660 km/h) at 21,325 ft (6 500 m); mission endurance (unrefuelled), 9 hrs at 620-mile (1 000-km) radius, 6 hrs at 1,240-mile (2 000-km) radius; service ceiling, 36,090 ft (11 000 m).

Weights: (Estimated) Normal max. take-off, 360,000 lb (163,290 kg).

Status: The Tu-126 AWACS aircraft is believed to have flown in prototype form in 1962–63 and first appeared in service with the Soviet Air Forces in the late 'sixties. Some 20–30 aircraft of this type are believed to be in service.

Notes: Essentially an adaptation of the Tu-114 commercial transport and retaining basically similar wings, tail surfaces power plant and undercarriage to those of the earlier aircraft, the Tu-126 is primarily intended to locate low-flying intruders and to vector interceptors towards them. The dominating feature of the aircraft is its pylon-mounted saucer-shaped early-warning scanner. The Tu-126 reportedly operates most effectively over water, possessing only limited overland "look-down" capability.

TUPOLEV TU-126 (MOSS)

Dimensions: Span, 168 ft 0 in (51,20 m); approx. length, 188 ft 0 in (57,30 m); height, 51 ft 0 in (15,50 m); wing area, 3,349 sq ft (311,1 m²).

TUPOLEV TU-144 (CHARGER)

Country of Origin: USSR.

Type: Long-range supersonic commercial transport.

Power Plant: Four 33,100 lb (15 000 kg) dry and 44,090 lb (20 000 kg) reheat Kuznetsov NK-144 turbofans.

Performance: Max. cruise, 1,550 mph (2 500 km/h) at altitudes up to 59,000 ft (18 000 m), or Mach 2·3; long-range cruise, 1,254 mph (2,018 km/h) at 52,490–55,775 ft (16 000–17 000 m), or Mach 1·9; max. range, 4,040 mls (6 500 km).

Weights: Operational empty, 187,395 lb (85 000 kg); max. take-off, 396,830 lb (180 000 kg).

Accommodation: Basic flight crew of three and maximum of 140 passengers in single-class arrangement with three-plus-two and two-plus-two seating.

Status: First pre-production aircraft (representative of production configuration) flown September 1971, and total of 20 (including pre-production aircraft) reportedly completed or nearing completion by beginning of 1978.

Notes: Technical problems, reportedly including excessive fuel consumption during cruise with partial reheat, delayed the introduction of the Tu-144 on regular passenger services until November 1, 1977, when Aeroflot initiated a regular service between Moscow and Alma Ata, mail and cargo flights having been made over this 2,190-mile (3 520-km) route by the aircraft on a more or less regular basis since December 26, 1975. The production standard Tu-144 shares little more than a generally similar configuration with the similarly-designated supersonic transport prototype flown for the first time on December 31, 1968. The photograph above (which depicts the ninth aircraft) shows the nose in the drooped position and the retractable "moustache" foreplanes extended.

TUPOLEV TU-144 (CHARGER)

Dimensions: Span, 91 ft 10⅓ in (28,00 m); length, 211 ft 5⅛ in (64,45 m); height, 42 ft 3 in (12,85 m); wing area, 4,714·6 sq ft (438 m²).

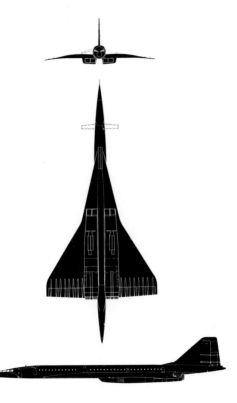

TUPOLEV TU-154B (CARELESS)

Country of Origin: USSR.

Type: Medium- to long-haul commercial transport.

Power Plant: Three 23,150 lb (10 500 kg) Kuznetsov NK-8-2U turbofans.

Performance: Max. cruise, 590 mph (950 km/h) at 31,000 ft (9 450 m); econ. cruise, 559 mph (900 km/h) at 36,090 ft (11 000 m); range (with max. payload—39,683 lb), 1,710 mls (2 750 km), (with 160 passengers), 2,020 mls (3 250 km), (with 120 passengers), 2,485 mls (4 000 km).

Weights: Max. take-off, 211,644 lb (96 000 kg).

Accommodation: Crew of three on flight-deck and basic arrangements for 160 single-class passengers in six-abreast seating, eight first-class and 150 tourist-class passengers, or (high density) 169 passengers.

Status: Prototype Tu-154 flown on October 4, 1968, current production model being the Tu-154B (introduced by Aeroflot in 1976) of which approximately four per month were being manufactured at the beginning of 1978. More than 200 Tu-154s (all versions) are currently in service with Aeroflot and the Tu-154B has also been supplied to Malev (three) of Hungary.

Notes: The Tu-154B combines the improvements introduced by the Tu-154A with major changes in controls and systems, and slight increases in weights. The wing spoilers have been extended in span and are now used for low-speed lateral control and passenger capacity has been increased by extending the usable cabin area rearwards, and an extra emergency exit has been added in each side of the fuselage. Various longer-range versions of the basic Tu-154 are known to be under study, including one reportedly powered by NK-86 turbofans similar to those of the Il-86.

TUPOLEV TU-154B (CARELESS)

Dimensions: Span, 123 ft 2½ in (37,55 m); length, 157 ft 1¾ in (47,90 m); height, 37 ft 4¾ in (11,40 m); wing area, 2,168·92 sq ft (201,45 m²).

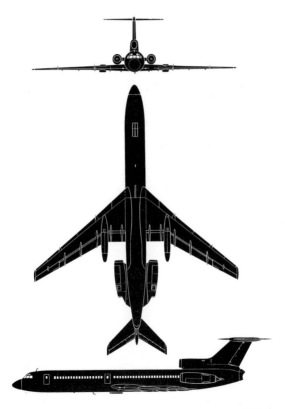

VALMET VIINKA

Country of Origin: Finland.

Type: Side-by-side two-seat primary trainer.

Power Plant: One 200 hp Avco Lycoming IO-360-A1B6 or AEIO-360-A1B6 four-cylinder horizontally-opposed engine.

Performance: Max. speed, 149 mph (240 km/h) at sea level; range (with max. payload), 534 mls (860 km); initial climb, 1,180 ft/min (6,0 m/sec); service ceiling, 18,045 ft (5 500 m).

Weights: Empty equipped, 1,521 lb (690 kg); max. take-off, 2,535 lb (1 150 kg).

Status: Prototype flown July 1, 1975, and production deliveries scheduled to commence early 1979 against Finnish Air Force order for 30 aircraft placed in November 1976.

Notes: The Viinka (Blast) was designed to meet the requirements of a specification drawn up by the Finnish Air Force and its cockpit provides space for an additional pair of seats or up to 661 lb (330 kg) of freight. The Viinka may also be adapted for the aeromedical role (with a single casualty stretcher and a medical attendant in addition to the pilot), for aerial photography and for glider towing, and the wheel undercarriage may be replaced by skis.

VALMET VIINKA

Dimensions: Span, 30 ft 6¼ in (9,30 m); length, 23 ft 11½ in (7,30 m); wing area, 150·69 sq ft (14,00 m²).

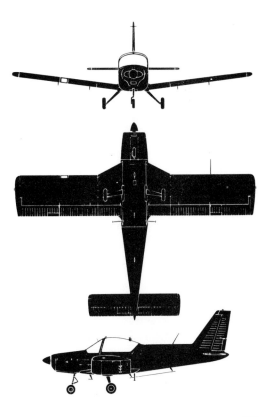

VFW-FOKKER VFW 614

Country of Origin: Federal Germany.

Type: Short-haul commercial transport.

Power Plant: Two 7,280 lb (3 302 kg) Rolls-Royce/SNECMA M45H Mk. 501 turbofans.

Performance: Max. speed, 457 mph (735 km/h) at 21,000 ft (6 400 m); max. cruise, 449 mph (722 km/h) at 25,000 ft (7 620 m); long-range cruise, 367 mph (591 km/h) at 25,000 ft (7 620 m); max. fuel range (with reserves), 1,249 mls (2 010 km); range (40 passengers and reserves), 748 mls (1 205 km); max. climb, 3,100 ft/min (15,75 m/sec); service ceiling, 25,000 ft (7 620 m).

Weights: Operational empty, 26,850 lb (12 180 kg); max. take-off, 44,000 lb (19 950 kg).

Accommodation: Basic flight crew of two and standard layout for 40 passengers in rows of four. Alternative arrangement for 44 passengers.

Status: First of three flying prototypes commenced test programme on July 14, 1971, with first production aircraft flying on April 28, 1975. This was delivered to Cimber Air in August 1975. Orders for 19 (two for Cimber Air, eight for Touraine Air Transport, three for Air Alsace, three for the Federal German government, one for the Romanian government and two for Tarom) recorded by end of 1977 when it was anticipated that further production would be terminated. Contract signed in June 1977 for manufacture of 97 in Romania (27 from German parts and remainder of completely Romanian manufacture) by Romavia was expected to be cancelled.

VFW-FOKKER VFW 614

Dimensions: Span, 70 ft 6½ in (21,50 m); length, 67 ft 7 in (20,60 m); height, 25 ft 8 in (7,84 m); wing area, 688·89 sq ft (64,00 m²).

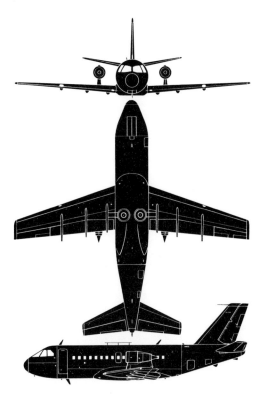

WSK-MIELEC M-15

Country of Origin: Poland.
Type: Single-seat agricultural aircraft.
Power Plant: One 3,307 lb (1 500 kg) Ivchenko AI-25 turbofan.
Performance: Max. cruise, 124 mph (200 km/h); normal operating speeds, 87–102 mph (140–165 km/h); endurance, 1·5 hrs (plus 30 min reserve); initial climb, 1,083 ft/min (5,5 m/sec).
Weights: Empty equipped, 6,393 lb (2 900 kg); max. take-off, 12,456 lb (5 650 kg).
Status: Aerodynamic prototype (LLP-M15) flown May 20, 1973, followed by first representative prototype on January 9, 1974. First batch of five of initial pre-production batch of 20 aircraft delivered to USSR for trials on April 26, 1975, and approximately 100 delivered to the USSR by mid-1977, with deliveries continuing at beginning of 1978.
Notes: The M-15 is unique in being the world's only turbofan-powered biplane. It is also one of the largest agricultural aircraft so far produced, the containers between the wings having a combined capacity of 4,850 lb (2 200 kg) of dry chemicals or 638 Imp gal (2 900 l) of liquid chemicals. The M-15 was evolved by a joint Polish-Soviet design team under the leadership of Kazimierz Gocyla to the requirements of a specification drawn up by the Soviet Ministry of Civil Aviation, and all production is currently being undertaken against orders from the USSR. Choice of biplane configuration was dictated by the need to maintain a low wing loading such as was demanded by the working speed despite a high take-off weight.

WSK-MIELEC M-15

Dimensions: Span, 73 ft 3⅛ in (22,33 m); length, 41 ft 8¾ in (12,72 m); height, 17 ft 6½ in (5,34 m); wing area, 723·33 sq ft (67,20 m²).

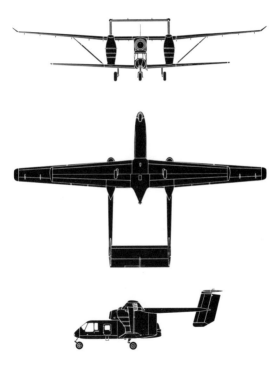

YAKOVLEV YAK-36MP (FORGER-A)

Country of Origin: USSR.
Type: Single-seat shipboard air defence and strike fighter.
Power Plant: One (approx.) 17,640 lb (8 000 kg) lift/cruise turbojet plus two 7,935 lb (3 600 kg) lift turbojets.
Performance: (Estimated) Max. speed, 695 mph (1 120 km/h) above 36,000 ft (10 970 m), or Mach 1·05, 725 mph (1 167 km/h) at sea level, or Mach 0·95; high-speed cruise, 595 mph (958 km/h) at 20,000 ft (6 095 m), or Mach 0·85; combat radius (internal fuel and 2,205-lb/1 000-kg external ordnance), 230 mls (370 km), (with two 110 Imp gal/500 l drop tanks, a reconnaissance pod and two AAMs), 340 mls (547 km); initial climb, 20,000 ft/min (101,6 m/sec).
Weights: (Estimated) Empty, 12,125 lb (5 500 kg); max. take-off, 22,000 lb (9 980 kg).
Armament: Four underwing pylons with total capacity of (approx.) 2,205 lb (1 000 kg), including twin-barrel 23-mm cannon pods, air-to-air missiles or bombs.
Status: The Yak-36MP (Forger-A) is believed to have flown in prototype form in 1971 and to have attained service evaluation status in 1976 aboard the carrier *Kiev*.
Notes: Possessing no short-landing-and-take-off (STOL) capability, being limited to vertical-take-off-and-landing (VTOL operation), the Yak-36 combines a vectored-thrust lift/cruise engine with fore and aft lift engines. The single-seat Yak-36MP possesses no attack radar and no internal armament. A tandem two-seat version, the Yak-36UV (Forger-B), has an extended forward fuselage.

216

YAKOVLEV YAK-36MP (FORGER-A)

Dimensions: (Estimated) Span, 24 ft 7 in (7,50 m); length, 52 ft 6 in (16,00 m); height, 11 ft 0 in (3,35 m); wing area, 167 sq ft (15,50 m²).

YAKOVLEV YAK-42 (CLOBBER)

Country of Origin: USSR.

Type: Short- to medium-haul commercial transport.

Power Plant: Three 14,320 lb (6 500 kg) Lotarev D-36 turbofans.

Performance: Econ. cruise, 510 mph (820 km/h) at 25,000 ft (7 600 m): range (max. payload—31,938 lb/14 500 kg), 620 mls (1 000 km), (with 26,430-lb/12 000-kg payload), 1,150 mls (1 850 km); max. range, 1,520 mls (2 450 km); time to cruise altitude (25,000 ft/7 600 m), 11 min.

Weights: Operational empty, 63,845 lb (28 960 kg); max. take-off, 114,640 lb (52 000 kg).

Accommodation: Basic flight crew of two and various alternative cabin arrangements, including 76 passengers in a mixed-class layout (16 first class), 100 passengers in a single-class layout with six-abreast seating and 120 passengers in a high-density layout.

Status: First prototype flown on March 7, 1975, followed by second in April 1976. A production prototype was flown in February 1977, and deliveries to Aeroflot are scheduled to commence during the first quarter of 1978.

Notes: The initial prototypes of the Yak-42 differed one from the other in wing sweep angle, the first prototype featuring 11 deg of sweepback and the second 25 deg, the latter sweep angle being adopted for production aircraft. The Yak-42 is intended for operation primarily over relatively short stages and utilising restricted airfields with poor surfaces and limited facilities in the remoter areas of the Soviet Union. Independent of airport ground equipment and having a heavy-duty undercarriage, the Yak-42 bears a close resemblance to the smaller Yak-40 (see 1977 edition).

218

YAKOVLEV YAK-42 (CLOBBER)

Dimensions: Span, 112 ft 2½ in (34,20 m); length, 119 ft 4 in (36,38 m); height, 32 ft 3 in (9,83 m); wing area, 1,615 sq ft (150,00 m²).

AÉROSPATIALE SA 319B ALOUETTE III

Country of Origin: France.
Type: Light utility helicopter (seven seats).
Power Plant: One 789 shp Turboméca Astazou XIVH turbo-shaft.
Performance: Max. speed, 137 mph (220 km/h) at sea level; max. cruise, 122 mph (197 km/h); max. inclined climb, 885 ft/min (4,49 m/sec); hovering ceiling (in ground effect), 10,170 ft (3 100 m), (out of ground effect), 5,575 ft (1 700 m); range (six passengers), 375 mls (605 km).
Weights: Empty, 2,442 lb (1 108 kg); max. take-off, 4,960 lb (2 250 kg).
Dimensions: Rotor diam, 36 ft 1¾ in (11,02 m); fuselage length, 32 ft 10¾ in (10,03 m).
Notes: The SA 319B is an Astazou-powered derivative of the Artouste-powered SA 316B Alouette III. All Alouette IIIs built prior to 1970 had the Artouste turboshaft, and approximately 1,400 Alouette IIIs (all versions) had been ordered by 71 countries by the beginning of 1978. Licence production has been undertaken in India, Romania and Switzerland. The naval version (illustrated) fulfils a variety of shipborne roles and for the ASW task may be fitted with search radar, MAD (Magnet Anomaly Detection) equipment and two Mk 44 homing torpedoes. The SA 319B may also be fitted with a gyro-stabilised sight and two wire-guided AS.12 or four AS.11 missiles for the anti-armour role.

AÉROSPATIALE SA 330J PUMA

Country of Origin: France.
Type: Medium transport helicopter.
Power Plant: Two 1,575 shp Turboméca IVC turboshafts.
Performance: Max. speed, 163 mph (262 km/h); max. continuous cruise at sea level, 159 mph (257 km/h); max. inclined climb, 1,400 ft/min (7,1 m/sec); hovering ceiling (in ground effect), 7,315 ft (2 230 m), (out of ground effect), 4,430 ft (1 350 m); max. range (standard fuel), 342 mls (550 km).
Weights: Operational empty, 10,060 lb (4 563 kg); max. take-off, 16,315 lb (7 400 kg).
Dimensions: Rotor diam, 49 ft 2½ in (15,00 m); fuselage length, 46 ft 1½ in (14,06 m).
Notes: The civil SA 330J and the equivalent military SA 330L were the current production models of the Puma at the beginning of 1978 when more than 540 Pumas of all versions had been ordered. The SA 330J and 330L differ from the civil SA 330F (passenger) and SA 330G (cargo), and SA 330H (military) models that immediately preceded them in having new plastic blades accompanied by increases in gross weights. The SA 330B (French Army), SA 330C (export) and SA 330E (RAF) had 1,328 shp Turmo IIIC4 turboshafts. Currently projected is the long-cabin SA 331 Puma to accommodate up to 26 persons and the SA 332 with 1,800 shp Turboméca Makila turboshafts. Components for the Puma are supplied by Westland in the UK.

AÉROSPATIALE SA 342 GAZELLE

Country of Origin: France.
Type: Five-seat light utility helicopter.
Power Plant: One 870 shp Turboméca Astazou XIVH turboshaft.
Performance: Max. speed, 193 mph (310 km/h); max. continuous cruise at sea level, 168 mph (270 km/h); max. inclined climb, 2,066 ft/min (10,5 m/sec); hovering ceiling (in ground effect), 13,120 ft (4 000 m), (out of ground effect), 10,330 ft (3 150 m); range at sea level, 488 mls (785 km).
Weights: Empty equipped, 2,114 lb (959 kg); max. take-off, 4,190 lb (1 900 kg).
Dimensions: Rotor diam, 34 ft $5\frac{1}{2}$ in (10,50 m); fuselage length, 31 ft $2\frac{3}{4}$ in (9,53 m).
Notes: The SA 342 is a more powerful derivative of the SA 341 (592 shp Astazou IIIA) and has been exported to Kuwait, Iraq and elsewhere, and is equipped to launch four HOT missiles, AS-11s or other weapons. A civil equivalent, the SA 342J offering a 220 lb (100 kg) increase in payload, became available in 1977, and sales of the SA 341 and 342 Gazelles exceeded 900 by the beginning of 1978. Versions of the lower-powered SA 341 comprise the SA 341B (British Army), SA 341C (British Navy), SA 341D (RAF), SA 341F (French Army), SA 341G (civil version) and SA 341H (military export version). Sub-assemblies are supplied by Westland, final assembly being by Aérospatiale.

AÉROSPATIALE AS 350 ECUREUIL

Country of Origin: France.
Type: Light general-purpose utility helicopter.
Power Plant: One 740 shp Turboméca Arriel or 592 shp Avco Lycoming LTS 101 turboshaft.
Performance: (Arriel turboshaft) Max. speed, 166 mph (267 km/h); max. continuous cruise at sea level, 143 mph (230 km/h); hovering ceiling (in ground effect), 10,660 ft (3 250 m), (out of ground effect), 8,200 ft (2 500 m); range, 430 mls (690 km).
Weights: Empty equipped, 2,094 lb (950 kg); max. take-off, 4,630 lb (2 100 kg).
Dimensions: Rotor diam, 35 ft 0¾ in (10,69 m); fuselage length, 35 ft 9½ in (10,91 m).
Notes: First (LTS 101-powered) Ecureuil (Squirrel) prototype flown on June 27, 1974, with second (Arriel-powered) following in February 1975. The Ecureuil is being offered with both the above-mentioned turboshafts and the first two of eight pre-series examples (both LTS 101-and Arriel-powered) were completed late in 1976 with the first customer deliveries scheduled for the first half of 1978. The standard production model is a six-seater and features include a Starflex all-plastic rotor head, simplified dynamic machinery and modular assemblies to simplify changes in the field. The Ecureuil is known in the USA as the AStar. Orders had been placed for some 200 by beginning of 1978, target output being 14 monthly.

AÉROSPATIALE SA 361 DAUPHIN

Country of Origin: France.
Type: Multi-purpose and transport helicopter.
Power Plant: One 1,282 shp Turboméca Astazou XX turbo-shaft.
Performance: Max. speed, 196 mph (315 km/h) at sea level; cruise, 175 mph (282 km/h) at sea level; max. inclined climb rate, 1,969 ft/min (10 m/sec); hovering ceiling (in ground effect), 13,450 ft (4 100 m), (out of ground effect), 10,990 ft (3 350 m); range, 425 mls (685 km).
Weights: Empty equipped, 3,487 lb (1 582 kg); max. take-off, 6,800 lb (3 300 kg).
Dimensions. Rotor diam, 38 ft 4 in (11,68 m); fuselage length, 36 ft 0½ (10,98 m).
Notes: The SA 361 is an overpowered version of the SA 360 (see 1977 edition) intended specifically for hot-and-high operating conditions. The military version, the SA 361H, can carry up to eight HOT (High-subsonic Optically-guided Tube-launched) anti-armour missiles, and deliveries of this helicopter (and its civil equivalent, the SA 361F) are scheduled to commence in the second half of 1978. Like the lower-powered SA 360, the SA 361 will accommodate up to 10 persons, and the slung load may be increased by 440 lb (200 kg) to 3,304 lb (1 500 kg). The first prototype Dauphin flew on June 2, 1972, with more than 30 delivered by 1978, and the prototype of the SA 361 version flew on July 12, 1976.

AÉROSPATIALE SA 365 DAUPHIN 2

Country of Origin: France.
Type: Multi-purpose and transport helicopter.
Power Plant: Two 680 shp Turboméca Arriel turboshafts.
Performance: Max. speed, 196 mph (315 km/h); max. continuous cruise at sea level, 163 mph (262 km/h); max. inclined climb rate, 1,653 ft/min (8,4 m/s); hovering ceiling (both in and out of ground effect), 15,000 ft (4 575 m); range, 339 mls (545 km).
Weights: Empty equipped, 3,980 lb (1 806 kg); max. take-off, 7,495 lb (3 400 kg).
Dimensions: Main rotor diam, 37 ft 8¾ in (11,50 m); fuselage length, 36 ft 3⅞ in (10,98 m).
Notes: First flown on January 24, 1975, with production deliveries commencing early in 1978, the SA 365 Dauphin 2 can accommodate up to 14 persons. Fitted with an all-plastic Starflex rotor head, the Dauphin 2 is offered for both civil and military roles, a proposed naval version having a nosewheel undercarriage, nose-mounted search radar, a gyro-stabilised weapons aiming sight, MAD (Magnetic Anomaly Detection) equipment and radio-command AS-15 anti-shipping missiles. A variant of the Dauphin 2, the SA 366 powered by two Avco Lycoming LTS101 turboshafts, was tested in prototype form but subsequently shelved and consideration is being given to a development of the helicopter with two uprated (730 shp) Arriel turboshafts.

AGUSTA A 109 HIRUNDO

Country of Origin: Italy.
Type: Eight-seat light utility helicopter.
Power Plant: Two 420 shp Allison 250-C20B turboshafts.
Performance: (At 5,402 lb/2 450 kg) Max. speed, 192 mph
(310 km/h); max. continuous cruise, 173 mph (278 km/h) at
sea level; hovering ceiling (in ground effect), 9,800 ft (2 987
m), (out of ground effect), 6,700 ft (2 042 m); max. inclined
climb, 1,600 ft/min (8,12 m/sec); max. range, 385 mls (620
km) at 148 mph (238 km/h).
Weights: Empty equipped, 2,998 lb (1 360 kg); max. take-
off, 5,402 lb (2 450 kg).
Dimensions: Rotor diam, 36 ft 1 in (11,00 m); fuselage
length, 36 ft 10$\frac{7}{8}$ in (11,25 m).
Notes: The first of four Hirundo (Swallow) prototypes flew
on August 4, 1971. A pre-production batch of 10 Hirundos
was followed by first customer deliveries late 1976. The
Hirundo is currently being offered for both civil and military
roles, five having been delivered to the Italian Army, including
two equipped to launch TOW (Tube-launched Optically-
tracked Wire-guided) missiles, one of these being illustrated
above. Proposed variants include a naval Hirundo with search
radar, gyro-stabilised weapons aiming sight and torpedo or
rocket armament, and the A 129 Mangusta (Mongoose) is a
projected light anti-armour helicopter utilising most of the
dynamic components of the A 109.

AGUSTA-BELL AB 212ASW

Country of Origin: Italy.

Type: Anti-submarine and anti-surface vessel helicopter.

Power Plant: One 1,290 shp (derated from 1,875 shp) Pratt & Whitney PT6T-6 coupled turboshaft.

Performance: (At 11,197 lb/5 080 kg) Max. speed, 122 mph (196 km/h) at sea level; max. cruise, 115 mph (185 km/h); max. inclined climb, 1,450 ft/min (7,38 m/sec); hovering ceiling (in ground effect), 12,500 ft (3 810 m), (out of ground effect), 4,000 ft (1,220 m); range (15% reserves), 414 mls (667 km) at sea level.

Weights: Empty equipped, 7,540 lb (3 420 kg); max. takeoff, 11,197 lb (5 080 kg).

Dimensions: Rotor diam, 48 ft 2½ in (14,69 m); fuselage length, 42 ft 10¾ in (13,07 m).

Notes: The AB 212ASW is an Italian anti-submarine derivative of the Bell 212 Twin Two-Twelve (see page 231) developed primarily for use by the Italian Navy (to which 28 examples are being delivered) and for export (batches having been delivered to Peru, Spain and Turkey). For the ASW mission, the AB 212ASW carried high-performance long-range search radar, ECM equipment, a gryo-stabilised sighting system and a pair of Mk 44 or Mk 46 homing torpedoes or depth charges. Agusta also manufactures the standard AB 212 and the AB 205 Iroquois, combined production rate being 12–15 monthly at the beginning of 1978.

BELL MODEL 206B JETRANGER III

Country of Origin: USA.
Type: Five-seat light utility helicopter.
Power Plant: One 420 shp Allison 250-C20B turboshaft.
Performance: (At 3,200 lb/1 451 kg) Max. speed, 140 mph (225 km/h) at sea level; max. cruise, 133 mph (214 km/h) at sea level; hovering ceiling (in ground effect), 12,700 ft (3 871 m), (out of ground effect), 6,000 ft (1 829 m); max. range (no reserve), 360 mls (579 km).
Weights: Empty, 1,500 lb (680 kg); max. take-off, 3,200 lb (1 451 kg).
Dimensions: Rotor diam, 33 ft 4 in (10,16 m); fuselage length, 31 ft 2 in (9,50 m).
Notes: Introduced in 1977, with deliveries commencing in July of that year, the JetRanger III differs from the JetRanger II which it supplants in having an uprated engine, an enlarged and improved tail rotor mast and more minor changes. Some 2,300 commercial JetRangers had been delivered by the beginning of 1978, both commercial and military versions (including production by licensees) totalling more than 5,000. A light observation version of the JetRanger for the US Army is designated OH-58A Kiowa and a training version for the US Navy is known as the TH-57A SeaRanger. The JetRanger is built by Agusta in Italy as the AB 206, and the JetRanger II has been built in Australia. A retrofit kit is available to bring earlier JetRangers to Srs.III standard.

BELL MODEL 206L LONGRANGER

Country of Origin: USA.
Type: Seven-seat light utility helicopter.
Power Plant: One 420 shp Allison 250-C20B turboshaft.
Performance: (At 3,900 lb/1 769 kg) Max. speed, 144 mph (232 km/h); cruise, 136 mph (229 km/h) at sea level; hovering ceiling (in ground effect), 8,200 ft (2 499 m), (out of ground effect), 2,000 ft (610 m); range, 390 mls (628 km) at sea level, 430 mls (692 km) at 5,000 ft (1 524 m).
Weights: Empty, 1,861 lb (844 kg); max. take-off, 4,000 lb (1 814 kg).
Dimensions: Rotor diam. 37 ft 0 in (11,28 m); fuselage length, 33 ft 3 in (10,13 m).
Notes: The Model 206L LongRanger is a stretched and more powerful version of the Model 206B JetRanger III, with a long fuselage, increased fuel capacity, an uprated engine and a larger rotor. The LongRanger is being manufactured in parallel with the JetRanger III and initial customer deliveries commenced in October 1975, prototype testing having been initiated on September 11, 1974. The LongRanger is available with emergency flotation gear and with a 2,000-lb (907-kg) capacity cargo hook. Cabin volume is 83 cu ft (2,35 m³) as compared with the 49 cu ft (1,39 m³) of the JetRanger III (see page 228). In the aeromedical or rescue role the Long-Ranger can accommodate two casualty stretchers and two ambulatory casualties.

BELL MODEL 209 HUEYCOBRA

Country of Origin: USA.

Type: Two-seat attack helicopter.

Power Plant: One (AH-1J) 1,800 shp Pratt & Whitney (Canada) T400-CP-400 or (AH-1T) 1,970 shp T400-WV-402 coupled turboshaft.

Performance: (AH-1J at 10,000 lb/4 535 kg) Max. speed, 207 mph (333 km/h) at sea level; max. inclined climb, 1,090 ft/min (5,54 m/sec); hovering ceiling (in ground effect), 12,450 ft (3 794 m); max. range (without reserves), 359 mls (577 km).

Weights: Empty equipped (AH-1J), 6,816 lb (3 091 kg), (AH-1T) 8,489 lb (3 854 kg); max. take-off (AH-1J), 10,000 lb (4 535 kg), (AH-1T), 14,000 lb (6 356 kg).

Dimensions: Rotor diam (AH-1J), 44 ft 0 in (13,41 m), (AH-1T) 48 ft 0 in (14,64 m); fuselage length, 44 ft 7 in (13,59 m).

Notes: The twin-engined (coupled turboshaft) version of the Model 209 is being produced in two versions, the first of these, the AH-1J, being essentially a "Twin Pac" powered version of the US Marine Corps' AH-1G SeaCobra (1,100 shp Lycoming T53-L-13), and in addition to being supplied to the USMC, this model is being manufactured for Iran (202 examples). The AH-1T (illustrated) flew in 1976 and differs in having the dynamic components of the Model 214 (see page 232), and delivery of 57 on order for the USMC commenced late in 1977.

BELL MODEL 212 TWIN TWO-TWELVE

Country of Origin: USA.

Type: Fifteen-seat utility helicopter.

Power Plant: One 1,800 shp Pratt & Whitney PT6T-3 coupled turboshaft.

Performance: Max. speed, 121 mph (194 km/h) at sea level; max. inclined climb at 10,000 lb (4 535 kg), 1,460 ft/min (7,4 m/sec); hovering ceiling (in ground effect), 17,100 ft (5 212 m), (out of ground effect), 9,900 ft (3 020 m); max. range, 296 mls (476 km) at sea level.

Weights: Empty, 5,500 lb (2 495 kg); max. take-off, 10,000 lb (4 535 kg).

Dimensions: Rotor diam, 48 ft $2\frac{1}{2}$ in (14,69 m); fuselage length, 42 ft $10\frac{3}{4}$ in (13,07 m).

Notes: The Model 212 is based on the Model 205 (see 1977 Edition) from which it differs primarily in having a twin-engined power plant (two turboshaft engines coupled to a combining gearbox with a single output shaft), and both commercial and military versions are being produced. A model for the Canadian Armed Forces is designated CUH-1N, and an essentially similar variant of the Model 212, the UH-1N, is being supplied to the USAF, the USN, and the USMC. All versions of the Model 212 can carry an external load of 4,400 lb (1 814 kg), and can maintain cruise performance on one engine component at maximum gross weight.

BELL MODEL 214B BIGLIFTER

Country of Origin: USA.

Type: Sixteen-seat utility helicopter.

Power Plant: One 2,930 shp Avco Lycoming T5508D turboshaft.

Performance: Max. speed, 190 mph (305 km/h) at sea level; max. cruise (at gross weight of 13,000 lb/5 897 kg), 150 mph (241 km/h); range, 300 mls (483 km).

Weights: Normal max. take-off, 13,000 lb (5 897 kg), (with slung load), 16,000 lb (7 257 kg).

Dimensions: Rotor diam, 50 ft 0 in (15,20 m).

Notes: Development of the BigLifter, originally known as the HueyPlus, was initiated in 1970 as a progressive development of the Model 205 (UH-1H). Utilising an essentially similar airframe with strengthened main beams, pylon structure and aft fuselage, and the main rotor and tail rotor drive systems of the Model 309 KingCobra (see 1973 edition) coupled with the Lycoming T55-L-7C turboshaft, this utility helicopter was developed for military use as the Model 214A and was certificated in 1975 for commercial use as the Model 214B. First flight of the Model 214A took place on March 13, 1974, and first deliveries against orders from the Iranian Government for 287 helicopters of this type (later supplemented by an order for a further six) began in April 1975 and were to be completed early 1978. Four hundred additional Model 214As are to be co-produced by Bell and the Iranian government.

BELL MODEL 222

Country of Origin: USA.

Type: Light utility and transport helicopter.

Power Plant: Two 650 shp Avco Lycoming LTS 101-650C turboshafts.

Performance: Max. cruise, 173 mph (278 km/h) at sea level; range cruise, 150 mph (241 km/h) at sea level; hovering ceiling (in ground effect), 13,000 ft (3 962 m), (out of ground effect), 8,200 ft (2 499 m); range (20 min reserve), 400 mls (644 km) at 8,000 ft (2 438 m).

Weights: Empty, 4,250 lb (1 928 kg); normal take-off, 7,200 lb (3 266 kg).

Dimensions: Rotor diam, 30 ft 0 in (11,89 m); fuselage length, 39 ft 9 in (12,12 m).

Notes: Designed to accommodate up to 10 persons (including pilot) in a high-density arrangement, with a standard interior providing eight seats and an executive six-seat layout, the Model 222 is the first US light twin-turbine helicopter and the first of five prototypes was flown on August 13, 1976, with production deliveries scheduled for early 1979. The Model 222 may be fitted with flotation gear or fixed skids as alternatives to the retractable tricycle wheel undercarriage, and kits will be available to adapt it for use in the aeromedical role, with accommodation for two casualty stretchers and two perambulatory casualties or medical attendants. Auxiliary vertical surfaces have now been added to the tailplane.

BOEING VERTOL MODEL 114

Country of Origin: USA.

Type: Medium transport helicopter.

Power Plant: (CH-47C) Two 3,750 shp Lycoming T55-L-11 turboshafts.

Performance: (CH-47C at 33,000 lb/14 969 kg) Max. speed, 190 mph (306 km/h) at sea level; average cruise, 158 mph (254 km/h); max. inclined climb, 2,880 ft/min (14,63 m/sec); hovering ceiling (out of ground effect), 14,750 ft (4 495 m); mission radius, 115 mls (185 km).

Weights: Empty, 20,378 lb (9 243); max. take-off, 46,000 lb (20 865 kg).

Dimensions: Rotor diam (each), 60 ft 0 in (18,29 m); fuselage length, 51 ft 0 in (15,54 m).

Notes: The Model 114 is the standard medium transport helicopter of the US Army, and is operated by that service under the designation CH-47 Chinook. The initial production model, the CH-47A, was powered by 2,200 shp T55-L-5 or 2,650 shp T55-L-7 turboshafts. This was succeeded by the CH-47B with 2,850 shp T55-L-7C engines, redesigned rotor blades and other modifications, and this, in turn, gave place to the current CH-47C with more powerful engines, strengthened transmissions, and increased fuel capacity. This model is manufactured in Italy by Elicotteri Meriodionali, orders calling for 24 (of 26) for the Italian Army, 8 for Libya and 18 (of 42) for the Iranian Army.

HUGHES 500M-D TOW DEFENDER

Country of Origin: USA.

Type: Light anti-armour helicopter.

Power Plant: One 420 shp Allison 250-C20B turboshaft.

Performance: (At 3,000 lb/1 362 kg) Max. speed, 175 mph (282 km/h) at sea level; cruise, 160 mph (257 km/h) at 4,000 ft (1 220 m); max. inclined climb, 1,920 ft/min (9,75 m/sec); hovering ceiling (in ground effect), 8,800 ft (2 682 m), (out of ground effect), 7,100 ft (2 164 m); max. range, 263 mls (423 km).

Weights: Empty, 1,295 lb (588 kg); max. take-off (internal load), 3,000 lb (1 362 kg), (with external load), 3,620 lb (1 642 kg).

Dimensions: Rotor diam, 26 ft 5 in (8,05 m); fuselage length, 21 ft 5 in (6,52 m).

Notes: The Model 500M-D is a multi-role military helicopter derived, via the civil Model 500D, from the US Army's OH-6A Cayuse observation helicopter. The TOW Defender version is an anti-armour helicopter with 7,62-mm armour for the crew, engine compressor and fuel control, and provision for four TOW (Tube-launched Optically-tracked Wire-guided) missiles. Various alternative weapons may be fitted, including seven-round launchers for 2.75-in rockets, a 30-mm chain gun on the fuselage side or a 7,62-mm chain gun in an extendible ventral turret. The Defender is being manufactured in South Korea under a co-production arrangement.

HUGHES YAH-64

Country of Origin: USA.

Type: Tandem two-seat attack helicopter.

Power Plant: Two 1,536 shp General Electric T700-GE-700 turboshafts.

Performance: Max. speed, 191 mph (307 km/h); cruise, 179 mph (288 km/h); max. inclined climb, 3,200 ft/min (16,27 m/sec); hovering ceiling (in ground effect), 14,600 ft (4 453 m), (outside ground effect), 11,800 ft (3 600 m); service ceiling, 8,000 ft (2 440 m); max. range, 424 mls (682 km).

Weights: Empty, 9,900 lb (4 490 kg); primary mission, 13,600 lb (6 169 kg); max. take-off, 17,400 lb (7 892 kg).

Dimensions: Rotor diam, 48 ft 0 in (14,63 m); fuselage length, 49 ft 4½ in (15,05 m).

Notes: Winning contender in the US Army's AAH (Advanced Attack Helicopter) contest, the YAH-64 flew for the first time on September 30, 1975. Two prototypes were used for the initial trials and three more with fully integrated weapons systems are under construction and scheduled to commence trials in first half of 1979, planned total procurement comprising 536 AH-64s. The AH-64 is armed with a single-barrel 30-mm gun based on the chain-driven bolt system and suspended beneath the forward fuselage, and eight BGM-71A TOW anti-armour missiles may be carried, alternative armament including 16 Hellfire laser-seeking missiles. Target acquisition and designation and a pilot's night vision systems will be used.

KAMOV KA-25 (HORMONE A)

Country of Origin: USSR.
Type: Shipboard anti-submarine warfare helicopter.
Power Plant: Two 900 shp Glushenkov GTD-3 turboshafts.
Performance: (Estimated) Max. speed, 130 mph (209 km/h); normal cruise, 120 mph (193 km/h); max. range, 400 mls (644 km); service ceiling, 11,000 ft (3 353 m).
Weights: (Estimated) Empty, 10,500 lb (4 765 kg); max. take-off, 16,500 lb (7 484 kg).
Dimensions: Rotor diam (each), 51 ft 7½ in (15,74 m); approx. fuselage length, 35 ft 6 in (10,82 m).
Notes: Possessing a basically similar airframe to that of the Ka-25K (see 1973 edition) and employing a similar self-contained assembly comprising rotors, transmission, engines and auxiliaries, the Ka-25 serves with the Soviet Navy primarily in the ASW role but is also employed in the utility and transport roles. The ASW Ka-25 serves aboard the helicopter cruisers *Moskva* and *Leningrad*, and the carrier *Kiev*, as well as with shore-based units. A search radar installation is mounted in a nose radome, but other sensor housings and antennae differ widely from helicopter to helicopter. There is no evidence that externally-mounted weapons may be carried. Each landing wheel is surrounded by an inflatable pontoon surmounted by inflation bottles. The Hormone-A is intended for ASW operations whereas the Hormone-B is used for over-the-horizon missile targeting.

MBB BO 105CB

Country of Origin: Federal Germany.
Type: Five/six-seat light utility helicopter.
Power Plant: Two 420 shp Allison 250-C20B turboshafts.
Performance: Max. cruise, 152 mph (245 km/h) at sea level;
max. inclined climb, 1,771 ft/min (9,0 m/sec); hovering ceiling
(in ground effect), 9,514 ft (2 900 m); normal range, 388 mls
(625 km) at 5,000 ft (1 525 m).
Weights: Empty, 2,360 lb (1 070 kg); max. take-off, 5,070
lb (2 300 kg).
Dimensions: Rotor diam, 32 ft 1¾ in (9,80 m); fuselage
length, 28 ft 0½ in (8,55 m).
Notes: The BO 105, of which more than 350 examples had
been delivered by the beginning of 1978, features a rigid un-
articulated main rotor and production deliveries commenced
in 1971, the current commercial version being described above,
this having an uprated engine by comparison with the BO 105C
(see 1977 edition). The Federal German Army is to receive 227
BO 105M/VBH helicopters for liaison and observation tasks
and 212 BO 105A/PAH anti-armour helicopters equipped with
HOT missiles. Deliveries to the Army are expected to commence in September 1978 and be completed by October 1982.
A larger helicopter, the BK 117 being developed jointly by MBB
and Kawasaki, will have much component commonality with
the BO 105 and will be an 8–12-seater. A prototype is planned
to fly mid-1979.

MIL MI-8 (HIP)

Country of Origin: USSR.

Type: General-purpose transport helicopter.

Power Plant: Two 1,500 shp Isotov TV-2-117A turboshafts.

Performance: (At 24,470 lb/11 100 kg) Max. speed, 155 mph (250 km/h); max. cruise, 140 mph (225 km/h); hovering ceiling (in ground effect), 5,900 ft (1 800 m), (out of ground effect), 2,625 ft (800 m); service ceiling, 14,760 ft (4 500 m); range with 6,615 lb (3 000 kg) of freight, 264 mls (425 km).

Weights: Empty (cargo), 15,787 lb (7 171 kg), (passenger), 16,352 lb (7 417 kg); normal take-off, 24,470 lb (11 100 kg); max. take-off (for VTO), 26,455 lb (12 000 kg).

Dimensions: Rotor diam, 69 ft 10¼ in (21,29 m); fuselage length, 59 ft 7⅓ in (18,17 m).

Notes: The Mi-8 has been in continuous production since 1964 for both civil and military tasks. The standard commercial passenger version has a basic flight crew of two or three and 28 four-abreast seats, and the aeromedical version accommodates 12 casualty stretchers and a medical attendant. As a freighter the Mi-8 will carry up to 8,818 lb (4 000 kg) of cargo, and military tasks include assault transport, search and rescue, and anti-submarine warfare. The Mi-8 is now operated by several Warsaw Pact air forces, serving primarily in the support transport role, and has been exported to numerous countries, including Finland, Pakistan and Egypt.

MIL MI-14 (HAZE-A)

Country of Origin: USSR.
Type: Amphibious anti-submarine helicopter.
Power Plant: Two 1,500 shp Isotov TV-2 turboshafts.
Performance: (Estimated) Max. speed, 143 mph (230 km/h); max. cruise, 130 mph (210 km/h); hovering ceiling (in ground effect), 5,250 ft (1 600 m), (out of ground effect), 2,295 ft (700 m); tactical radius, 124 mls (200 km).
Weights: (Estimated) Max. take-off, 26,455 lb (12 000 kg).
Dimensions: Rotor diam, 69 ft 10$\frac{1}{4}$ in (21,29 m); fuselage length, 59 ft 7 in (18,15 m).
Notes: The Mi-14 amphibious anti-submarine warfare helicopter, which serves with shore-based elements of the Soviet Naval Air Force, is a derivative of the Mi-8 (see page 239) and employs essentially similar power plant and dynamic components, and much of the structure is common between the two helicopters. New features include the boat-type hull, outriggers which, housing the retractable lateral twin-wheel undercarriage members, incorporate water rudders, a search radar installation beneath the nose and a sonar "bird" beneath the tailboom root. The Mi-14 may presumably be used for over-the-horizon missile targeting and for such tasks as search and rescue. It may also be assumed that the Mi-14 possesses a weapons bay for ASW torpedoes, nuclear depth charges and other stores. This amphibious helicopter reportedly entered service in 1975.

MIL MI-24 (HIND-D)

Country of Origin: USSR.
Type: Assault and anti-armour helicopter.
Power Plant: Two 1,500 shp Isotov TV-2 turboshafts.
Performance: (Estimated) Max. speed, 160 mph (257 km/h); max. cruise, 140 mph (225 km/h); hovering ceiling (in ground effect), 6,000 ft (1 830 m), (out of ground effect), 1,600 ft (790 m); normal range, 300 mls (480 km).
Weights: Normal take-off, 22,000 lb (10 000 kg).
Dimensions: Rotor diam, 55 ft 0 in (16,76 m); fuselage length, 55 ft 6 in (16,90 m).
Notes: The Hind-D version of the Mi-24 assault helicopter embodies a redesigned forward fuselage and is optimised for the gunship role and has tandem stations for the weapons operator (in the extreme nose) and pilot with individual canopies, the cockpit of the latter being raised to afford an unobstructed forward view. A four-barrel Gatling-type large-calibre machine gun is mounted in an offset chin turret, there are four wing pylons for rocket pods (32×55-mm) and end-plate pylons at the wingtips carry rails for four Swatter anti-tank missiles. Apart from the Hind-D, the principal service versions of the Mi-24 are the Hind-A (see 1977 edition) armed assault helicopter featuring a flight deck for a crew of four, and the essentially similar Hind-C which has no nose gun and undernose sighting system, or missile rails at wingtips. The Hind-C and Hind-D are apparently complementary.

SIKORSKY S-61D (SEA KING)

Country of Origin: USA.
Type: Amphibious anti-submarine helicopter.
Power Plant: Two 1,500 shp General Electric T58-GE-10 turboshafts.
Performance: Max. speed, 172 mph (277 km/h) at sea level; inclined climb, 2,200 ft/min (11,2 m/sec); hovering ceiling (out of ground effect), 8,200 ft (2 500 m); range (with 10% reserves), 622 mls (1 000 km).
Weights: Empty equipped, 12,087 lb (5 481 kg); max. take-off, 20,500 lb (9 297 kg).
Dimensions: Rotor diam, 62 ft 0 in (18,90 m); fuselage length, 54 ft 9 in (16,69 m).
Notes: A more powerful derivative of the S-61B, the S-61D serves with the US Navy as the SH-3D (illustrated above), 72 helicopters of this type following on production of 255 SH-3As (S-61Bs) for the ASW role for the US Navy, four being supplied to the Brazilian Navy and 22 to the Spanish Navy. Four similar aircraft have been supplied to the Argentine Navy as S-61D-4s and 11 have been supplied to the US Army/ US Marine Corps Executive Flight Detachment as VH-3Ds. Licence manufacture of the S-61D is being undertaken in the United Kingdom (see pages 248–9), in Japan for the Maritime Self-Defence Force and in Italy by Agusta for the Italian and Iranian navies. The SH-3G and SH-3H are upgraded conversions of the SH-3A.

SIKORSKY S-61R

Country of Origin: USA.
Type: Amphibious transport and rescue helicopter.
Power Plant: (CH-3E) Two 1,500 shp General Electric T58-GE-5 turboshafts.
Performance: (CH-3E at 21,247 lb/9 635 kg) Max. speed, 162 mph (261 km/h) at sea level; range cruise, 144 mph (232 km/h); max. inclined climb, 1,310 ft/min (6,6 m/sec); hovering ceiling (in ground effect), 4,100 ft (1 250 m); range with 10% reserves, 465 mls (748 km).
Weights: (CH-3E) Empty, 13,255 lb (6 010 kg); normal take-off, 21,247 lb (9 635 kg); max. take-off, 22,050 lb (10 000 kg).
Dimensions: Rotor diam, 62 ft 0 in (18,90 m); fuselage length, 57 ft 3 in (17,45 m).
Notes: Although based on the S-61A, the S-61R embodies numerous design changes, including a rear ramp and a tricycle-type undercarriage. Initial model for the USAF was the CH-3C with 1,300 shp T58-GE-1 turboshafts, but this was subsequently updated to CH-3E standards. The CH-3E can accommodate 25–30 troops or 5,000 lb (2 270 kg) of cargo, and may be fitted with a TAT-102 barbette on each sponson mounting a 7,62-mm Minigun. The HH-3E is a USAF rescue version with armour, self-sealing tanks, and refuelling probe, and the HH-3F Pelican (illustrated) is a US Coast Guard search and rescue model, an Agusta licence-built example being illustrated.

SIKORSKY S-65 (YCH-53E)

Country of Origin: USA.

Type: Amphibious assault transport helicopter.

Power Plant: Three 4,380 shp General Electric T64-GE-415 turboshafts.

Performance: Max. speed, 196 mph (315 km/h) at sea level; max. cruise, 173 mph (278 km/h).

Weights: Operational empty, 33,000 lb (14 968 kg); max. take-off, 69,750 lb (31 638 kg).

Dimensions: Rotor diam., 79 ft 0 in (24,08 m); fuselage length, 73 ft 5 in (22,38 m).

Notes: The YCH-53E is a growth version of the CH-53D Sea Stallion (see 1974 edition) embodying a third engine, an uprated transmission system, a seventh main rotor blade and increased rotor diameter. The first of two prototypes was flown on March 1, 1974, and the first of two pre-production prototypes flew on December 8, 1975, but a production decision was not anticipated prior to 1978. The YCH-53E can accommodate up to 56 troops in a high-density arrangement and can lift a 32,000-lb (14 515-kg) external load over a radius of 58 miles (93 km) at sea level in a 90 deg F temperature. The planned production programme envisages the acquisition of 70 helicopters of this type divided equally between the US Navy and US Marine Corps. The YCH-53E offers a major performance advance and can retrieve 93 per cent of USMC tactical aircraft without disassembly.

SIKORSKY S-70 (UH-60A) BLACK HAWK

Country of Origin: USA.

Type: Tactical transport helicopter.

Power Plant: Two 1,543 shp General Election T700-GE-700 turboshafts.

Performance: Max. speed, 224 mph (360 km/h) at sea level; cruise, 166 mph (267 km/h); vertical climb rate, 450 ft/min (2,28 m/sec); hovering ceiling (in ground effect), 10,000 ft (3 048 m), (out of ground effect), 5,800 ft (1 758 m); endurance 2·3–3·0 hrs.

Weights: Design gross, 16,500 lb (7 485 kg); max. take-off, 22,000 lb (9 979 kg).

Dimensions: Rotor diam, 53 ft 8 in (16,23 m); fuselage length, 50 ft 0¾ in (15,26 m).

Notes: The Black Hawk was winner of the US Army's UTTAS (Utility Tactical Transport Aircraft System) contest, and contracts had been announced by beginning of 1978 for 71 examples with deliveries commencing August 1978. The first of three YUH-60As was flown on October 17, 1974, and a company-funded fourth prototype flew on May 23, 1975. The Black Hawk is primarily a combat assault squad carrier, accommodating 11 fully-equipped troops, but it is capable of carrying an 8,000-lb (3 629-kg) slung load and can perform a variety of secondary missions, such as reconnaissance and troop resupply. Commercial versions of the Black Hawk were under study at the beginning of 1978.

SIKORSKY S-70L

Country of Origin: USA.
Type: Shipboard multi-role helicopter.
Power Plant: Two 1,630 shp General Electric T700-GE-400 turboshafts.
Performance: (Estimated) Max. cruise, 172 mph (277 km/h); max. vertical climb rate, 450 ft/min (2,28 m/sec); ceiling, 10,000 ft (3 050 m); time on station (at radius of 57 mls/92 km), 3 hrs, (at radius of 173 mls/278 km), 1 hr.
Weights: Mission loaded (ASW), 19,377 lb (8 789 kg), (anti-ship surveillance), 17,605 lb (7 985 kg).
Dimensions: Rotor diam, 53 ft 8 in (16,36 m); fuselage length, 50 ft 0¾ in (15,26 m).
Notes: The S-70L was selected by the US Navy on September 1, 1977, as winning contender in its LAMPS (Light Airborne Multi-purpose System) Mk. III helicopter, the first of five proto-types being scheduled to fly in December 1978, and the US Navy having a requirement for more than 200 helicopters of this type, with deliveries commencing in 1981. The S-70L (which is expected to receive the service designation SH-60B) is a derivative of the UH-60A Black Hawk and will be capable of carrying two homing torpedoes, 25 sonobuoys and an exten-sive range of avionics. It will serve aboard DD-963 destroyers, DDG-47 Aegis cruisers and FFG-7 guided-missile frigates as an integral extension of the sensor and weapons system of the launching vessel.

SIKORSKY S-76

County of Origin: USA.
Type: Fourteen-seat commercial transport helicopter.
Power Plant: Two 700 shp Allison 250-C30 turboshafts.
Performance: Max. speed, 179 mph (288 km/h); max. cruise, 167 mph (268 km/h); range cruise, 145 mph (233 km/h); hovering ceiling (in ground effect), 5,100 ft (1 524 m), (out of ground effect), 1,400 ft (427 m); range (full payload and 30 min reserve), 460 mls (740 km).
Weights: Empty, 4,942 lb (2 241 kg); max. take-off, 9,700 lb (4 399 kg).
Dimensions: Rotor diam, 44 ft 0 in (13,41 m); fuselage length, 44 ft 1 in (13,44 m).
Notes: The first of four prototypes of the S-76 flew on March 13, 1977, and planning at the beginning of 1978 called for customer deliveries to commence in July with a production rate of seven per month being attained by January 1979. The S-76 is unique among Sikorsky commercial helicopters in that conceptually it owes nothing to an existing military model, although it has been designed to conform with appropriate military specifications and military customers were included among contracts for 92 helicopters of this type that were claimed to have been placed at the time flight testing commenced. The S-76 may be fitted with extended-range tanks, cargo hook and rescue hoist, and a version has been proposed to meet a US Coast Guard requirement.

WESTLAND SEA KING MK. 2

Country of Origin: United Kingdom (US licence).
Type: Anti-submarine warfare and search-and-rescue helicopter.
Power Plant: Two 1,500 shp Rolls-Royce Gnome 1400-1 turboshafts.
Performance: Max. speed, 143 mph (230 km/h); max. continuous cruise at sea level, 131 mph (211 km/h); hovering ceiling (in ground effect), 5,000 ft (1 525 m), (out of ground effect), 3,200 ft (975 m); range (standard fuel), 764 mls (1 230 km), (auxiliary fuel), 937 mls (1 507 km).
Weights: Empty equipped (ASW), 13,672 lb (6 201 kg), (SAR), 12,376 lb (5 613 kg); max. take-off, 21,000 lb (9 525 kg).
Dimensions: Rotor diam, 62 ft 0 in (18,90 m); fuselage length, 55 ft 9¾ in (17,01 m).
Notes: The Sea King Mk 2 is an uprated version of the basic ASW and SAR derivative of the licence-built S-61D (see page 241), the first Mk 2 being flown on June 30, 1974 and being one of 10 Sea King Mk 50s ordered by the Australian Navy. Twenty-one have been ordered for the Royal Navy as Sea King HAS Mk 2s and 15 examples of a SAR version have been ordered by the RAF as Sea King HAR Mk 3s, these being scheduled to enter service during the first quarter of 1978. A total of 202 Westland-built derivatives of the S-61D (including Commandos) had been ordered by the beginning of 1978.

WESTLAND COMMANDO MK. 2

Country of Origin: United Kingdom (US licence).
Type: Tactical transport helicopter.
Power Plant: Two 1,590 shp Rolls-Royce Gnome 1400-1 turboshafts.
Performance: Max. speed (at 19,900 lb/9 046 kg), 138 mph (222 km/h); max. cruise, 127 mph (204 km/h); max. inclined climb, 1,930 ft/min (9,8 m/sec); range (with 30 troops), 161 mls (259 km); ferry range, 1,036 mls (1 668 km).
Weights: Empty equipped, 11,487–12,122 lb (5 221– 5 510 kg); max. take-off, 20,000 lb (9 072 kg).
Dimensions: Rotor diam, 62 ft 0 in (18,89 m); fuselage length, 54 ft 9 in (16,69 m).
Notes: The Commando is a Westland-developed land-based army support helicopter derivative of the licence-built Sikorsky S-61D Sea King (see page 242), search radar and other specialised items being deleted together with the sponsons which endow the Sea King with amphibious capability. The first five examples completed as Commando Mk. 1s were minimum change conversions of Sea King airframes, the first of these flying on September 12, 1973, but subsequent Commandos are being built to Mk. 2 standards with the uprated Gnome turboshafts selected for the Sea King Mk. 50s ordered by Australia. The first production deliveries (to Egypt) commenced in 1975, that illustrated being a VIP transport.

WESTLAND WG.13 LYNX

Country of Origin: United Kingdom.
Type: Multi-purpose, ASW and transport helicopter.
Power Plant: Two 900 shp Rolls-Royce BS.360-07-26 Gem 100 turboshafts.
Performance: Max. speed, 207 mph (333 km/h); max. continuous sea level cruise, 170 mph (273 km/h); max. inclined climb, 1,174 ft/min (11,05 m/sec); hovering ceiling (out of ground effect), 12,000 ft (3 660 m); max. range (internal fuel), 391 mls (629 km); max. ferry range (auxiliary fuel), 787 mls (1 266 km).
Weights: (HAS Mk 2) Operational empty, 6,767–6,999 lb (3 069–3 174 kg); max. take-off, 9,500 lb (4 309 kg).
Dimensions: Rotor diam, 42 ft 0 in (12,80 m); fuselage length, 39 ft 1¼ in (11,92 m).
Notes: The first of 13 development Lynxes was flown on March 21, 1971, with the first production example (an HAS Mk 2) flying on February 10, 1976. By the beginning of 1978, when some 35 had been completed, production rate was four per month and 223 were on order, including 26 for the French Navy, 60 for the Royal Navy, 100 for the British Army, seven for the Danish Navy, nine for the Brazilian Navy and 16 for the Netherlands Navy. Production tempo is expected to attain 11 monthly in 1979. The Lynx AH Mk 1 is the British Army's general utility version and the Lynx HAS Mk 2 is the ASW version for the Royal Navy.

ACKNOWLEDGEMENTS

The author wishes to record his thanks to the following sources of copyright photographs appearing in this volume: Aviation Magazine International, pages 150 and 152; Paul R. Duffy, page 78; Flug Revue International, pages 154 and 198; Koku Fan, page 158; Howard Levy, page 26; Stephen Peltz, pages 168 and 180; Gianni Siccardi, page 6. The three-view silhouette drawings published in this volume are copyright Pilot Press Limited and may not be reproduced without prior permission.

INDEX OF AIRCRAFT TYPES

Printed for the Publishers by

Butler & Tanner Ltd, Frome and London

2662.1177